D0097723

TRUE COLORS

JIM TALLEY
TERRY BENNER

TRUE
COLORS

❖ *A Janet Thoma Book* ❖

THOMAS NELSON PUBLISHERS
Nashville

Published in Nashville, Tennessee, by Thomas Nelson, Inc., and distributed in Canada by Lawson Falle, Ltd., Cambridge, Ontario.

Scripture quotations are from the NEW KING JAMES VERSION of the Bible. Copyright © 1979, 1980, 1982, Thomas Nelson, Inc., Publishers.

Scripture quotations marked NAS are from the THE NEW AMERICAN STANDARD BIBLE, Copyright © 1960, 1962, 1963, 1968, 1971, 1972, 1973, 1975, 1977 by The Lockman Foundation and are used by permission.

Scripture quotations marked (NIV) are taken from The Holy Bible: NEW INTERNATIONAL VERSION. Copyright © 1978 by the New York International Bible Society. Used by permission of Zondervan Bible Publishers.

Library of Congress Cataloging-in-Publication data
Talley, Jim A.
    True colors / Jim Talley and Terry Benner.
      p. cm.
    ISBN 0-8407-7579-2
    1. Witness bearing (Christianity) 2. Spiritual life—Baptist authors.
I. Benner, Terry. II. Title.
BV4520.T34   1991
248.4—dc20   91-4151
                                             CIP

Printed in the United States

1 2 3 4 5 6 7 8 97 96 95 94 93 92 91

CONTENTS

PART ONE: Revealing Your True Colors

1. A Chameleon is Born   *1*
2. Animal Identification   *16*
3. Walk a Mile in My Shoes   *33*

PART TWO: Custom Colors

4. The Fellowship Chameleon   *57*
5. The Financial Chameleon: Using Jesus Christ as Collateral   *77*
6. The Romantic Chameleon   *93*
7. The Leadership Chameleon: Make a Decision and We'll Follow You Anywhere!   *114*

PART THREE: Peeling Off the Paint

8. With Time, Patience, and a Well-Tuned Piano, Eventually, the Colors Fade *141*
9. Learning the Notes: Practice, Practice, Practice *167*
10. Healing the Wounds *185*
11. Restoring the Colors *198*

PART ONE

REVEALING YOUR TRUE COLORS

Chapter 1

A CHAMELEON IS BORN

I HAVE THIS problem with things that have scales and tend to slither. It's not exactly a phobia but it trots close to the edge.

When I was in kindergarten one of the kids brought his pet lizard to school. Lester was his name—the lizard's, not the kid's. As soon as they saw Lester and his owner appear through the doorway, some of my bolder classmates were suddenly very anxious to expand their scientific knowledge by performing certain "hands–on" experiments on Lester, such as seeing how far his tail would stretch and checking the degree of bulge in his eyes when his neck was squeezed.

I, for one, was quite content to observe from afar, always with something substantial between Lester and me. Usually the most substantial thing I could find was Mrs. Hildamyer, my teacher. I knew Mrs. Hildamyer was the teacher because she was in charge of bathroom-going and graham-cracker-distribution, two powerful and awe-inspiring responsibilities. Anyone in charge of food distribution and waste disposal in a kindergarten classroom had to have her act together. She would obviously know how to handle Lester if he became a rogue lizard and attacked with no warning.

Over the next couple of days, I was to find that Lester had a unique talent; a fascinating, endearing talent; a talent that caused even those of us with marshmallow souls to draw near with wonder. Lester belonged to that special part of the lizard family known as chameleons.

Chameleons can change their color to approximate whatever color they might be near. Matching its surroundings allows the chameleon camouflage from its enemies. Its ability to blend in also hides it from unsuspecting insects that crawl within easy reach of its long and sticky tongue, allowing it to bring about their swift, bewildered demise.

To us the lizard was magical. We were amazed to be a part of that magic, even control it, because we could determine Lester's color by changing his surroundings. The different colors seemed to wash across his reptilian ugliness and make it disappear, or at least become acceptable. He consistently fulfilled our expectations, thus gaining our trust. Because his ability to change color was not only enticing but seemingly under our control, he slithered his way right into our hearts.

A few years ago I was reminded of Lester's unique talent after almost thirty years of not giving him a thought.

I was sitting across from a woman, Andrea, after teaching a Sunday school class on the subject of forgiveness. She began sharing with me her struggle to forgive her ex-husband. I asked her about those things he had done during their three-year marriage that she could not bring herself to forgive. I'll never forget her words.

"It's not the things that happened during the marriage that I struggle with," Andrea said. "It's what took place before the marriage. You see, this was my second marriage. My first husband was an unbeliever and it led to our divorce. I promised myself and the Lord that if I ever married again it would be to a Christian man. He would be a man who had made Jesus Christ his Lord and Savior and was growing in his walk.

"After about a year of attending the singles' class at my church, I met this wonderful man." Her eyes glistened. "The first time I went out with him he shared his testimony and how much the Lord meant to him. He was active at his church; he talked about his helping on several committees. I knew he was the kind of man I was looking for. We began dating, attending church together, and even praying together. When he asked me to marry him I just knew that the Lord had put this man in my life."

"He sounds like a great man," I interjected. "What was the problem?"

"For the first few months after the wedding things seemed fine. Before long, though, I began to notice subtle changes in Tom. He spoke less and less about the Lord, when it seemed we used to talk about Him all the time. When we were first married we prayed together regularly, but by the time we'd been married six months our prayer life had dwindled to anemic blessings before meals.

"Tom began to miss Sunday school and, eventually, I found myself attending worship service alone. Within a year after we were married, there was no sign that the Lord had ever been a part of his life. And two and a half years after we had taken our wedding vows, my Christian husband was involved with another woman."

As tears started to form in her eyes Andrea said, "It's not Tom's infidelity or failure as a husband that I can't forgive, but how he used my love for the Lord as a key to open my heart. I feel as though there is no one I can trust now. It's bad enough that there are people in the body of Christ capable of doing this, but it frightens me that pastors can be fooled into putting these people into positions of spiritual leadership. If this is all the church has to offer, I might as well go back to the world; at least there, I know what to expect."

That night as I thought about what she had

shared, I realized that Andrea's pain and frustration were understandable. She felt betrayed, not only by someone who professed to know Christ, but by the church. The church had opened its doors to Tom, and even welcomed him into positions of leadership. Why hadn't anyone noticed—especially the church's other leaders—that this man was something other than what he appeared? How had no one seen his true colors?

They had all encountered a spiritual chameleon.

The Delivery Room

All of us who claim Jesus Christ as Savior and Lord, and have submitted our lives to Him, have a chameleon living within us; that is, in most areas of our lives we want to appear more wise, understanding, forgiving, and spiritually motivated than we really are. We want to hide or disguise weakness, pride, rebellion, and just general cussedness from others. This is part of our sin nature, the dark side of our humanity.

We come to Christ because we are tired of the world, tired of our lives, and tired of our sin. We may have had some hopes and dreams, some expectations of what our lives were going to be like, but they have ended up in a trash compactor somewhere.

The world is in the business of distributing

a product called inadequacy. In great detail it shares with us what the "successful person" is like, teases us with the idea that we could be that person, and then allows us to struggle to become what is an impossible dream.

At some point we uncover the lie and discover the truth of Proverbs 14:12: "There is a way that seems right to a man,/ But its end is the way of death." We're on that road. We now know it's a dead end, but we can't find the exit sign.

Then, someone comes into our life and shares the good news of Jesus Christ. There is a way leading to life, and we learn it begins with Him. We accept this marvelous gift of salvation, this redirecting of our lives that begins by giving us new freedom. The past loses its deed of ownership.

All of our struggles and failures, our guilt and shame may not disappear, but the way we think and feel about ourselves changes. The stranglehold of our past loosens; we now have a chance to write a new story for ourselves. We feel fresh, clean, and alive for the first time, and we have great expectations of what a tremendous experience life is going to be from now on.

And why shouldn't we feel that way? The person who first shared with us spoke of how God had done fantastic things in his life, and the people at church seem so enthusiastic and spiritually alive. We're excited to think that what has happened in their lives can happen in ours.

After a while we begin to realize that, like the world, many churches have their own definition of a "successful person" that places demands on us, just as burdensome as the ones the world heaped on our shoulders. We're expected to attend morning and evening worship services and a Sunday school class. We're expected to share our faith and have quiet time, prayer time, and time in the Word. We're expected to clean up our language, change our friends, and have a joyful attitude about it all. The one thing we're not expected to do is fail.

On the pages of this new and sparkling clean story we start recording failures. Anger, lust, envy, greed: they're all still there, only now we seem to notice them more quickly. They appear larger than life, especially as we work and worship next to so many saints. Where is the joy everyone keeps talking about? Why are we not as fervent or happy as others? Why are we not changing like everyone else? This brother recovered from alcohol, that couple salvaged their marriage, and we're having trouble turning off the TV long enough to have a quiet time.

We feel inadequate, now struggling more than ever. We're supposed to be victors, overcomers, conquerors, but we feel like failures. Sound familiar? Whatever a successful Christian is, obviously we are not, so we compensate. We decide to blend into our surroundings, to become, at least on the surface, what the expectations demand. We change our colors until we display the aura of spiritual success. In other words, we start to fake it.

Success in the world is hard to counterfeit. Good looks, money, or power are all fairly external. People either see that you have them or they don't. We have learned, however, that success as a Christian is determined by what is happening inside and is easier to imitate as long as we remain a safe distance from others. All we must do is show up on Sunday, smile, share something spiritual, or just sit and nod our heads with a knowing and appreciative expression as someone else shares with us. For a little while on Sunday morning, our lives are no longer shades of gray. We've stepped into a world of color, and we take on those colors, not to purposely deceive or mislead anyone, but to feel accepted and a part of things, to pretend for a while that we haven't failed again.

Welcome to the delivery room where spiritual chameleons are born.

Hiding Because of Fear

Every Christian, whether brand new or twenty years old in the Lord, has moments as a spiritual chameleon. It may last only an instant and be for the most innocent reasons, or it may span a lifetime and be driven by selfish and destructive needs. I have been a spiritual chameleon from the moment of my spiritual birth.

I had prayed the prayer of salvation. The prayer room counselor looked across the table at me. Was I sure that my sins were forgiven? Was I washed clean by the blood of Christ? Was He living in my heart right now? Actually, I wasn't all that certain. But the poor guy had sweated and shared and prayed with me in that little room for close to thirty minutes. I didn't have the heart—I was hopeful Jesus was living there—to let him down, so I said, "Yes, I'm sure."

Over the next several weeks, all that I had said I was sure of was validated. But for a few minutes at the very hour of my birth, I pretended to have more spiritual maturity than I had, not for any malicious or dishonest reason, but simply because I was concerned for a fellow human being.

As the years passed and I continued my walk with the Lord, the chameleon which took its first breath that day was like a shadow on a sunlit morning, a presence that walked hand in hand with my insecurities and inadequacies as a Christian.

We read in 1 Peter 1:15, 16 that we are called to be holy as God is holy. We strive but fall short, ashamed of our failure. Anxious that if other members of the body of Christ saw us with all of our conflicts and blemishes we would not be acceptable, we mask and obscure our deficiencies.

Every believer has these tendencies; for some, they become a way of spiritual life.

Jill had been a Christian for two years. Before accepting Christ she had been very shy and withdrawn. The Lord had made some extraordinary changes in her life, and in the safety of her Sunday school class or Bible study group, she loved to tell people about them. But she still struggled with sharing her testimony with strangers and had not found the courage to do so.

Some of the people in her Bible study had been Christians for only a few months, yet had shared repeatedly with others. One had even brought a co-worker to Christ. Because of this inadvertent but earnest pressure, Jill began to change color to blend with her spiritual environment. She joined in the conversation with statements like, "Yes, it is difficult to share with family" or, "There's nothing like the experience of bringing someone to Christ," leaving the impression that she was sharing her faith. It was not her desire to use or mislead anyone, just to be accepted.

If failure and guilt were the only consequences of taking on the habits of a chameleon, then the spiritual damage might be contained within our own lives. But given the proper nurture and habitat, the chameleon within can grow into a dragon. We discover that spiritual credentials can help us realize some desire. By imitating a spiritual nature, we continue to hide our true colors, and our camouflage becomes more elaborate.

A Pretense of Righteousness

If we allow the pretense of spiritual righteousness to continue without recognizing, confessing, and repenting of our sin, as James 5:16 calls us to do, then the reality and lordship of Christ begins to diminish in our life. Within our old nature, a trove of lusts and desires moves us in a never-ending quest for physical and emotional satisfaction, fulfilled by people or things existing outside of ourselves. The intensity of this quest is directly related to the reality of Jesus Christ in our lives. The more we focus on pleasing Him and less on gratifying ourselves, the more real He is to us. As we seek Him less, His reality in our lives diminishes, the old lusts and desires begin to dominate our thoughts and actions. Our focus shifts from pleasing God to pleasing ourselves, giving birth to another variety of spiritual chameleon.

As we move away from Him and closer to our old nature, the talent we have acquired at hiding becomes a tool used to meet the demands of our old self, to which we are giving more and more attention. Whereas we once hid out of shame and frustration for not measuring up to the "successful Christian" image, we begin to disguise ourselves out of a directed passion to meet those demands, with little or no regard for the spiritual impact on others.

Maybe we are single and want a romantic relationship; we are in business and desire more customers; we want to lead and have never been allowed; we are lonely and simply want friends. The body of Christ becomes a colossal resource for satisfying these needs. It is not that these desires are so terrible. In fact, most of them are quite acceptable, even worthy. The abuse is in pretending to be something we aren't in order to attain these goals.

When Christians use the colors of a relationship with Christ as a tool to manipulate fellow believers, the body of Christ ceases to serve as a haven from the world. The church will no longer provide a special environment where trust and honesty allow us to let down our guard—show our true colors—and relax in the comfort of fellow believers. The conscience of the chameleon will become calloused. Ultimately, people may even begin to question whether or not they have ever known Jesus Christ as Lord and Savior.

This may be a rather harsh and frightening indictment: that every day, members of the body of Christ, just like the woman in my Sunday school class, are in danger of being pulled back into the world, into spiritual oblivion, because they have trusted and been disappointed by chameleons unwilling to turn around and follow Christ.

Show Your True Colors

After eighteen years for Jim and ten for me in the ministry of singles at Modesto First Baptist Church, we have come to the conclusion that our fears are often focused upon the wrong things. It is not the deceit of the world but the fraud within our own lives that will wash across us and quench the Spirit of God. Maintaining an effective witness before the world of the miraculous changing power of the gospel requires personal integrity in our relationships with Christ and with those in the body of Christ. We are not seeking superspirituality. We follow Christ, while dealing honestly with the sin and failures in our lives, enabling others to do the same. We want to prevent needless pain in relationships, especially among Christians. Thus, we believe God wants us to be very careful about what we, as Christians, become comfortable with in our relational and spiritual commitments.

As you move through the pages of this book, there are some things to keep in mind. First, all of us have a tendency to change colors. Your pastor's spouse may tell you that the person you see during the week is not the spiritual paragon the congregation is blessed with on Sunday. We might not be hiding any ongoing sin, but we may imply that we are much stronger spiritually than we really are.

Also, we may continue too long in this innocent pretense. Our innocence is often presumed by others and we fail to correct them. Silence is not truth. If this happens, there is a danger that we will start believing our pretense, establishing in our minds an image of spiritual maturity that we will want to protect. The longer we live with this false image, the more comfortable it will become, and the more uncomfortable we will become with the lordship of Christ. Christ always brings the light of truth into our lives, exposing what is false—the very thing chameleons try desperately to disguise.

As we feed and care for this false spiritual image, we are also nurturing that creature called spiritual pride. It must have more than someone else. We begin to compare ourselves with other believers; we want to be more, have more. C. S. Lewis said, "A proud man is always looking down on things and people; and, of course, as long as you are looking down, you cannot see something that is above you." We find that the more mature image we project, the more people will trust us, seek our company, our leadership, even our counsel. Wrapped in a garment of bright spiritual colors, this acts as a relational vehicle into the inner circle of others' lives.

Finally, we become aware that our camouflage can do much more than protect. We can use it to satisfy certain ambitions and desires that have taken center stage since Christ became an extra. The chameleon, once just a frightened little reptile, has mutated so often we have lost our very sense of spiritual personality.

Only as we become more intimate with Jesus Christ will we see tendencies that seem normal to the world—and at times acceptable to the church—develop scales, long tails, and sharp claws that can wound our faith and the faith of others.

Changing spiritual colors is apt to be one of the more prevalent obstacles in the life of the believer, and one of the most difficult to recognize, for himself, his friends, and those in spiritual authority over him.

This book is about the chameleon that exists in us all. How do we recognize it in ourselves and others? How do we protect ourselves from becoming a chameleon or the victim of one? And how do we help the chameleons in our midst?

Identification, eradication, protection, restoration: these hold the keys to true-color Christian living.

Chapter 2

ANIMAL IDENTIFICATION

STARTING LIFE WITH a new wife and a new house was a real challenge. Jo Ann and I moved into a new house a few years ago. Within a few weeks we were barraged with all sorts of innovative sales presentations, one of which was particularly intriguing.

The representative from a local company that sold water softening units visited us one afternoon. The first step of his presentation was to test some pure bottled water, free of contaminants. The salesman put three drops of a particular chemical into it, and we sat and watched it turn a bright pink.

"This," he said rather smugly, "is what

drinking water should look like if it has the ideal mineral concentration."

Naturally, the water he tested from our tap turned a foreboding purple. The salesman shook his head slowly and, just under his breath, let out a low "uh-oh."

There were six different tests. Each time he used the pure water first to show us what the chemical reaction should be. Then he would show us the noxious color our water became with the same test. The effect would not have been nearly as dramatic had we not first been shown what the ideal should be. Without that constant to contrast with, the ominous purple would not have looked as menacing; in fact, we might have assumed the color was entirely acceptable.

By the fifth or sixth test, I no longer had to check the pure water sample. That bright pink had ground itself into my memory, and I needed only to look at the comparison sample to tell if the water was good. The more familiar we became with the standard, the easier it was to recognize the unacceptable.

Only as we become more intimate with Jesus Christ will we see tendencies that seem normal to the world—and at times acceptable to the church—turn into the scales, long tails, and sharp claws that can wound our faith and the faith of others.

Ideally, if you are growing as a Christian, you are becoming intimately familiar with the Water of Life, Jesus Christ, and as I describe the characteristics of the spiritual chameleon, they will seem as unsatisfactory and distasteful as that purple water did to Jo Ann and me.

The Script

The first trait that helps to identify the chameleon is that he speaks and acts as if he were following a script. He usually has the spiritually correct response with the customary spiritual language. He seldom has an awkward moment, as if everything were choreographed. The script is dictated by the circumstances and environment.

If the chameleon finds himself in a Bible study with little sharing or vulnerability, he will be content to operate at that level quite comfortably. If he is part of a study that shares more deeply and more openly, then he will express more concern and share at that same level, but only those things with which he is very secure; he will be very selective. It is unlikely that he will share a sin or weakness that is not under his control, that seems alien to the others, or will separate him from the group in any way.

Even if the group becomes critical or tends to gossip, he will be agreeable as long as it appears to be the accepted behavior. Because he survives by reading and responding to those around him, he seldom initiates a new direction;

nor does he attempt to stretch or confront the group. There is a lack of spiritual insight, of original spiritual thought. Instead, he is like a tape recorder giving back only what it has heard.

He will avoid making decisions and taking action in situations where he could appear ignorant or spiritually inadequate. It isn't that the chameleon doesn't like to give advice; he loves to, but only where he feels safe. The situation inviting his response must be very general where ecclesiastical cliches will suffice. If someone shares that he lacks joy in his spiritual walk, the chameleon may counter with, "You must be in the Word for the joy to be in you," or, "If you're not spending time with God, He can't spend time with you."

A friend of mine, Dennis Shaeffer, calls this "cheap and dirty advice." The chameleon finds tact preferable to asking direct and focused questions, such as "How much time do you spend in the Word?" "What do you think the Lord is saying to you?" "How are you praying, what are you praying about?" "Is there sin in your life that you have not dealt with?" "How can I help?" These questions require specific answers from one person and specific suggestions from the chameleon. The honest and sincere response to these inquiries forces the chameleon into a closer relationship with that person, and may require that he minister to this person in some way.

Ministering to another has a way of bonding us to that person. In a way, their successes and failures become ours. The Christian can deal with this identification because his self-image is a product of understanding his worth to God. His relationship with Christ puts a spiritual hedge around his self-image.

The chameleon operates in just the opposite way. His self-image depends on how he perceives himself in other people's eyes, not on God's unconditional love. How well liked is he, how admired, how popular? Failure of any kind affects that self-image, and consequently threatens his self-worth.

Bob had signed up for our Wednesday night "Living For Christ" class, which has the goal of teaching and preparing people to share their faith in a variety of circumstances. The first few weeks are spent in the classroom using lecture, group discussion, and role-playing. During the remainder of the class a new person is paired with a trainer, and they are given an opportunity to share their faith by calling on people in the community who have visited the church. Bob, though not a member of the church, was a friend of Susan's and had been coming to Sunday school for several months. On many occasions he had mentioned to Susan how much he enjoyed sharing his faith, so she invited him to the class.

During the group discussions Bob was an integral part of the class, sharing insights, stories and personal experiences, leading the group to believe that evangelism was a natural part of his

life. After a few months, however, his trainer began to notice that Bob had been absent several
times. These absences seemed to coincide with
those evenings when role-playing was to take
place.

During role-play one student would take
the part of a nonbeliever, usually with a specific
difficulty or attitude, and another student would
attempt to share their faith. There was no script,
but there was a variety of valuable approaches and
techniques that the students were learning to use.
Naturally, sometimes the student playing the
nonbeliever would get into the part and, in fun,
make it a bit difficult for the one doing the sharing.

Many students, during the course of the
first few weeks, had talked about their hesitancy to
share their faith, and for them, as well as for some
of us who were trainers, the role-playing was an
intimidating experience. In spite of their fear and
uncertainty, and sometimes because of it, they
stayed with the program. Bob did not. As soon as
we began going out on home visits Bob dropped
the class, stepped out of Susan's life, and disap-
peared, not in a blaze of color but over a rather
drab horizon.

It wasn't fear that made Bob a chameleon;
it wasn't dropping the class or even his decision to
quit attending church. It was his efforts to establish spiritual credentials—a fraudulent spiritual
attitude and philosophy. Had it not been for that

class Bob may have established himself, not only in the singles' group and the church, but in Susan's life as well. And had Bob been successful in establishing those credentials, avenues of leadership within the singles' ministry would have opened to him, and a path into Susan's heart may not have been far behind.

Seldom will you find the chameleon caught in the spotlight where there is only black and white, right or wrong. He prefers to immerse himself in shadowy areas where the most popular words are "possibly," "supposedly," and "perhaps." That is his protection. If you can avoid the appearance of being wrong, then people assume you must be right. As long as the chameleon is allowed to operate in areas where the grading system is always on a curve, he can continue to appear quite wise and mature.

God's Word has very little gray in it as Hebrews 4:12 will attest: "For the word of God is living and powerful, and sharper than any two-edged sword, piercing even to the division of soul and spirit, and of joints and marrow, and is a discerner of the thoughts and intents of the heart."

The chameleon usually has very little to do with God's Word for light reveals true colors. Instead, the chameleon uses Scripture sparingly, only a dab here and there, just enough to break up the solid silhouette of who he truly is.

Clean and Efficient

Because they become only tools of camouflage, there is no thirst of the heart for the things of Christ. The chameleon's second characteristic is that he makes clean and efficient use of what he spiritually possesses. He finds that it takes very little to convince others of the maturity of his walk. A few memory verses are all that's necessary if they are of such a general nature that they can be used in most situations.

An emotional testimony is usually a part of the chameleon's beautiful spiritual color. It is a testimony characterized by dramatic mistakes, followed by complete brokenness which often results in a miraculously changed life. I do not mean, in any way, to make light of sincere testimonies of this nature. They are examples of God's amazing and miraculous intervention into hurting and lost lives. They are used of God in a mighty way, witnessing to a lost world and encouraging and exhorting those of us who are already saved.

It is this very power of the personal testimony that validates the chameleon's spiritual credentials. However, in Matthew 7:22,23 Christ warns, "Many will say to Me in that day, 'Lord, Lord, have we not prophesied in Your name, cast out demons in Your name, and done many wonders in Your name?' And then I will declare to them, 'I never knew you; depart from Me, you who practice lawlessness!' "

The chameleon may not cast out demons or perform miracles, but he may bring a kind of implied spiritual power to his testimony with statements like, "It's a miracle I'm here today," or "I'm living proof that God can give tremendous victory in a life." The chameleon's testimony usually takes place somewhere else and involves people and circumstances difficult to verify; at the same time it is one of the most effective ways to validate his relationship with the Lord. People can argue about doctrine and take exception to your interpretation of Scripture, but they cannot discount your testimony for it is yours alone. This makes it powerful in witnessing but powerful in deceiving also.

When a chameleon is allowed the throne of a believer's life, time in the Word, personal prayer, and quiet meditation are all excess baggage; they serve no purpose. These things come from the inner heart's thirst to know more intimately the Lord and Savior to whom we have given our lives. They arise from the desire to change and to grow so that we might please and honor the One who has given us so much. That close relationship is nonexistent in the chameleon's life and so is the thirst. No one sees or appreciates the changes of the heart except Christ, so they have no effective function for the chameleon. Because he cannot experience the essence of the Christian's daily walk, he lives it vicariously. He listens to what others share about their experience with Christ, fits it to his own circumstances, and then gives it back to the group as a personal experience.

The aspect of being clean and efficient affects how the chameleon relates to others. He usually has no close, same-sex friends. I am not talking about casual friends who share some common interest that causes you to spend time together, such as tennis, fishing, yearbooks, etc. The chameleon might have quite a few of these, which are safe and seem to satisfy the need for companionship, but he has no close or intimate same-sex friends within the body of Christ.

Any sense of intimacy is difficult for the chameleon to develop with members of the same sex, because romantic love and the haze of romance—missing in a same-sex friendship—are essential ingredients which can dazzle a person, allowing the chameleon to step in much closer than would otherwise be possible. A man will be much more objective about his male friends than he will be about his female friends and vice versa.

Close friendship requires that there be an unconditional aspect to it. The intimate friend says, "I will be here in the good times and the bad. I will comfort you, encourage you, and when necessary confront you. I will be vulnerable with you and share my hopes and dreams, my heartaches and my sins. I will pray for you and with you, hold you accountable, and I will expect the same from you." To ask the chameleon to have an intimate friend is like asking an embezzler to open the account books.

The chameleon, however, will approach the opposite sex with the express need for a friend—a confidant, someone who understands and is easy to talk to. The other person will tend to be more open and vulnerable and begin to share problems and struggles—an unhappy childhood, conflict at work, a bitter divorce. The chameleon will show tremendous empathy and may share similar experiences, which leads the friend to believe she has found someone "who really understands."

The chameleon will give no sound counsel and offer few solutions, avoiding any implication that the other may share the blame, again staying in the gray areas. Instead, he will encourage an atmosphere of self-pity and the "Oh woe is me!" syndrome or, in this case, "Oh woe is us!" This fosters an attitude of "us against them." Later, when others urge caution in the relationship, the chameleon's response will be, "They haven't suffered as we have. How can they possibly understand?"

There is truth in the old saying "misery loves company," and there are many Christians who, if you whisper sympathetic words in their ear, will follow you anywhere.

Hiding in the Acceptable

The third mark of the chameleon is that he seldom challenges the status quo. A chameleon seeking a leadership position will be very accepting of the prevailing environment until he establishes himself. In group situations he always agrees with those he feels are mature Christians. He does not want to bring attention to himself, especially negative attention. He gives ardent verbal support to most ministry programs, and seldom questions the established, accepted policies and procedures unless he feels threatened. He is more secure in his environment if he knows what to expect. He is like a blind man, constantly tapping a cane before him, making sure it's safe before taking the next step.

Although the chameleon becomes adept at hiding his heart and his soul, he has no inhibition about manifesting his spiritual presence, seeking involvement in the ministries which offer higher visibility.

The group functions as a reassuring, protective womb for emotional testimony, diluted prayer, and pseudo-spiritual small talk. It protects him because few Christians will confront or even question in a group setting. Those with a timid nature assume that anyone who speaks so easily and intensely must be spiritually mature. There is a tendency not to question or confront the validity or sincerity of what the chameleon says,

thereby avoiding an uncomfortable situation. Besides, what the chameleon shares is often valid,
regardless of its hypocrisy.

Because it is difficult to find fault with what
the chameleon says, the group tends to favor him.
Although he may only rehash what has been said
before, there may be many who are impressed if
hearing it for the first time. Because what he says
has validity, people will feel obliged to agree and
share heartfelt, authenticating incidents from
their own lives.

The chameleon might say, "You know,
some time ago I found that I need at least twenty
to thirty minutes alone with the Lord each day or I
feel dry and empty inside. I would challenge everyone here to make your quiet time not a habit
but a need in your life." With this statement he
accomplishes three things: He establishes his own
spiritual credentials in terms of an acceptable
spiritual function; he enhances the group's perception of his closeness with the Lord by hinting
that, while he may stumble occasionally, his failure is the exception rather than the rule; finally,
by challenging the group, he puts himself in the
role of a teacher or temporary spiritual authority.

You won't hear the chameleon make this
statement, "You know, I am really struggling in
my walk these days. I've not had a quiet time in
two weeks, and it's been more than a month since
I read the Word. When I do have prayer time it's

really superficial. I just don't know what to do. Can somebody help me?" What brings a Christian to this point is the vast emptiness he feels in being separated from his Lord. Pride, popularity, respect, and admiration are finally swept away in his frustrated weariness of feeling spiritually alone.

The Christian has the experiential wisdom of remembering, with the heart, what it was like to have a familiar relationship hour-by-hour with Jesus Christ. This memory enhances and intensifies the destitution of living in a spiritual world of pretend. Nothing matters except regaining what he once had.

The chameleon feels none of this and is seldom pushed by his heart's conviction to this innermost revelation of his spiritual character.

All of these attributes are of a generic nature, touching all types of chameleons. They may, however, take on a slightly different look or feel depending on the type of chameleon, and how far the chameleon has moved from being a cute little lizard to a mature dragon.

After reading this chapter our natural tendency is to slide these characteristics across our friends, acquaintances, even our spouses, but not across ourselves. Jim and I have decided to help you look in the mirror instead of out the window. For your benefit we have created what we call the Scales and Tails Test, to help you decide if you've just hatched out of the egg or have grown large enough to go in search of a few knights to devour.

The Scales and Tails Test

    1. When was the last time you shared your testimony with a nonbeliever without any other believers present?

    2. How often in the last week have you spent time alone with the Lord, reading His Word and talking with Him? How many of your friends would believe this time to be more than it is?

    3. How much difference is there between how people perceive your spiritual life and what your spiritual life is?

    4. Do you spend a significant amount of time comparing your spiritual maturity with that of others? Do you feel either subtle pride or hopeless inadequacy as a result?

    5. Are you in a romantic relationship with another Christian? Are you willing to honestly share your spiritual inadequacies, spiritual fears, and spiritual failures with this person?

    6. If you were to lose your title or position of authority in your church or ministry, do you feel you would be less significant spiritually? Do you feel others would see you as less significant?

    7. Do you tend to exaggerate what is happening in your life spiritually?

    8. When was the last time you shared with a

friend a spiritual failure or ongoing struggle? Have you been able to move out from under its control?

9. Have you ever asked a Christian to step into a financial agreement that you would not have felt comfortable asking a non–believer to consider?

10. If you were to die tonight, do you know beyond a shadow of a doubt that you would spend eternity with the Lord? If not, have you shared this doubt with someone who can help?

11. Do you find there are only certain areas in your church where you are willing to serve? Do you most often serve where you feel comfortable? Do you frequently help in ministries that are highly visible?

12. Do you find yourself behaving differently in terms of what you talk about, the interests you have, and the important things in your life, depending upon whether you are with mature Christians, brand new Christians, or non-Christians?

13. Are you more aggressive in sharing mature spiritual insight or counsel and giving comfort to individuals of the opposite sex than you are with the people of the same sex?

Some, if not all, of these questions will probably make you feel a little uneasy, maybe very uneasy. I would be surprised if they didn't. They make me feel uneasy as I write them. That's because in each of us is a compulsion to show only what we feel makes us acceptable. If this self-examination makes you feel uncomfortable, chances are the lizard is still pretty small. If you got through the questions with hardly a blink of an eye, then you may be starting to believe your own camouflage.

Chapter 3

WALK
A MILE
IN MY
SHOES

I HATE MURDER mysteries. I can never figure out who did it. For me it is an exercise in mental futility. The worst part, however, is the last page of the book; I dread getting there. There, all is revealed, including the fact that, when it comes to deductive reasoning, I function somewhere between a mentally deficient chicken and an intelligent earthworm. My choice of who did it is usually arrived at with the same straightforward logic that people use to pick lottery numbers.

When people become romantically involved with and then marry spiritual chameleons, there comes a time when they reach the last page of the mystery. They can finally identify the villain —it's the person sitting across the breakfast table from them. They can now look back at all the clues, some subtle, some not so subtle, that they completely missed. But the real tragedy is that they can finally identify themselves as the victim. I assume that most people function somewhat better than an intelligent earthworm. Why, then, do we have so many victims? What is it about their mind-set and spiritual discernment that makes them more susceptible to the chameleon's camouflage?

Before we begin a discussion on the characteristics of a victim there is one ground rule that must be established. The victims we are talking about are Christians who are walking with the Lord and growing in their faith. They have a commitment to the lordship of Jesus Christ and their life reflects that commitment. Lack of spiritual maturity is not usually the issue. I don't believe it is a significant revelation that people who are not walking with the Lord and growing in their faith will make poor choices, not only relationally but in every area of their life. It does not take a spiritual chameleon's guise to fool those who are already spiritually blind. What is it, however, that clouds the vision of those who are not?

The Spiritually Naive

One Sunday I was sitting in church and happened to look across the aisle at two of my acquaintances. I am fairly sure they did not know each other and just happened to sit down together. One was a single middle-aged woman who attended church every Sunday morning but was involved in little else. Her husband had left her the year before, and the anger and hurt that she felt was slowly turning into bitterness. She would not forgive her husband for leaving her, or God for allowing it to happen. She came to church out of a lifelong habit, but sat in the pew worshiping her Lord with a spiteful spirit and a calloused heart.

Beside her sat a young woman who had been involved in our missions program for the past couple of years and would soon be going to Niger to work in a leprosy clinic. She was a trained occupational therapist and would be using her skills that she might share the gospel with those who needed not only her medical knowledge, but even more importantly, her knowledge of the Lord Jesus Christ.

As I sat looking at those two individuals—both claiming Jesus Christ as Savior, both part of the body of Christ, and both apparently worshiping their Lord—I realized how wide the boundaries of the kingdom are. The unconditional love and ongoing grace of the King are truly amazing. The only difference between those who continue to move toward the center of the kingdom and closer to the King, and those who tiptoe just inside the boundary, is the width of an open heart and the depth of a grateful soul.

The naive Christian would look at these two women and make the assumption that, because they were both in the same spot geographically on Sunday morning, they were in the same spot spiritually; that because they were both in church they were of equal sincerity, that they had the same intellectual and emotional commitment to the lordship of Jesus Christ. The assumption of the naive Christian is that most people who attend church consistently are spiritually mature beings, that their physical presence in the house of God somehow validates that they have all had the same spiritual experience.

It is a quirk of human nature to assume that how I go, so goes the world. If I am happy, everyone should be happy. If I am content, everyone should be content. This same tendency taints our spiritual perceptions. It is especially evident in Christians who have had a healthy, growing relationship with Christ for several years but have done little discipling or ministry work. They lack a realistic vision of the Christian environment, of how wide the boundaries of the kingdom can be. The assumption is that if I am a Christian and you are a Christian then we have a common level of experience and commitment.

Denise was a young woman who had accepted Christ several years earlier and consistently grown in her faith and her personal relationship with Christ. She had been involved in Bible studies, Sunday school, and our Living for Christ class, so that sharing her faith had become a way of life. As her faith matured she became more involved in ministry, serving on committees and being a faithful servant wherever the need arose. Slowly but surely, she moved up through various levels of leadership.

Eventually she was asked to coordinate our women's prayer room counseling program, which placed her at a high level of ministry involvement and responsibility. Part of that responsibility was meeting once a month with other ministry coordinators and the singles' pastor to discuss ministry plans, be involved in training, and give input on the various concerns of the ministry. During this meeting we discussed the people involved in the different ministries. Were there any special needs in that individual's life? Did we know of any spiritual problems that needed to be dealt with before allowing someone into the first levels of leadership, before delegating to them more responsibility?

By the end of the meeting Denise was reacting emotionally to what she heard: the progress of a young man she had known and worked with in ministry for the past year, divorced because he had been convicted of sexually abusing his eight–year–old daughter; a recovering alcoholic whose ex-wife had called because he was beating on her front door in the middle of the night, demanding to be let in; the young couple who had just received Christ but were living together unwed, insisting it was OK because God had obviously brought them together.

I am not saying that these people were insincere in their faith, nor am I implying that they were chameleons. I am saying that if a person has not worked in ministry areas comforting, encouraging, confronting, and exhorting fellow believers they can, like Denise, have a very naive view of the body of Christ.

The naive Christian says, "What Christ has done in my life He has done in yours. If I hunger to be with the Lord, it must be the same with you. If pleasing Him is the most important thing in my life, it must also be for you. If, in the security of the Lord's love, I am willing to share my weaknesses and failures so that others might help me, then that must be a desire of your heart."

Once these assumptions are made, many of our natural defenses are lowered, and our willingness to trust and be vulnerable increases dramatically.

Unconditional Love Vs. Unconditional Acceptance

Believers who confuse agape love with romantic love find that their spiritual commitment to the other person becomes entangled in their relational commitment. In this process the characteristics of agape love become warped and twisted.

In 1 Corinthians 13:7 Paul says that love "always protects, always trusts, always hopes, always perseveres" (NIV). This is God's love, agape love, which offers a protective womb of grace, forgiveness, and power that surrounds us, within which we can grow and prosper spiritually. But it is also a love that confronts and disciplines. Hebrews 12:6–10 says, " 'For whom the LORD loves He chastens,/And scourges every son whom He receives.' If you endure chastening, God deals with you as with sons; for what son is there whom a father does not chasten? But if you are without chastening, of which all have become partakers, then you are illegitimate and not sons. Furthermore, we have had human fathers who corrected us, and we paid them respect. Shall we not much more readily be in subjection to the Father of spirits and live? For they indeed for a few days chastened us as seemed best to them, but He for our profit, that we may be partakers of His holiness."

It is a love that has direction and purpose. The direction is to move us closer and closer to the likeness of Jesus Christ. The purpose is to make us lights in a dark world so that others may find their way to the Son. Jesus commands us to love others with this same love: "A new commandment I give to you, that you love one another; as I have loved you, that you also love one another" (John 13:34).

Romantic love is different from agape love in both direction and purpose. The direction of romantic love moves two people closer together physically and emotionally. The purpose of romantic love is to sustain the relationship no matter what. As a result, forgiveness becomes a blank check we give to each other without the bookkeeping of confrontation and accountability.

We protect the other person without insisting on confession, forgiveness, and repentance, and ignoring or rationalizing that which we know is wrong in the other person's life. It's as though we use the excuse of agape love—which is unconditional *love* and not unconditional *acceptance*—as a way to soften the rough edges or cover the cracks and holes in another's life, especially when we would rather not deal with issues that could jeopardize the relationship.

She says, "Yes, I know he loses his temper a lot, but he's under pressure at work." Translation: "That's not really a claw, it's just a sharp fingernail."

He says, "As soon as she finds out what her spiritual gifts are and where God would like her to serve, she'll jump right in." Translation: "I know she eats flies, but I'm sure her diet will change soon."

She says, "I know he has some weak areas,

but I'm sure God is working on them. We just need to be patient." Translation: "I know he's got a long tail, but if we just watch it long enough, it will get shorter."

In each of the above statements the error is not dealt with in terms of helping the person recognize and deal with the problem, as does the love of God. Instead, the problems are either justified, rationalized, or dismissed as being less serious than they really are. That, many times, is what relational love does. Often we allow romantic love to masquerade as God's love. We tolerate sin without repentance in the name of forgiveness. We justify spiritual dryness in the name of patience. We excuse rebellion under the label of an open mind and a compassionate heart.

The victim mistakenly believes that she is responding according to God's will, while every decision to excuse and ignore puts one more coat of camouflage paint on the chameleon's body. Hebrews 4:12 says, "For the word of God is living and powerful, and sharper than any two-edged sword, piercing even to the division of soul and spirit, and of joints and marrow, and is a discerner of the thoughts and intents of the heart." It is a shame that we sometimes turn this sword of God into a butter knife and use it to spread frosting over areas in our lives God would have us uncover.

Using the Church's Standard and Not the Lord's

Many people approach Scripture in the same way they approach a tax form: constantly in search of the elusive loophole. Where's the boundary line and how close can I get before someone calls foul? I think one of the most tedious and nonproductive counseling sessions for a pastor is time spent with someone who insists on searching through Scripture to find verses that justify either what they have done or what they want to do. I don't believe the writers of Scripture ever intended, or even imagined, that people who claimed the blood of the Lamb would attempt to manipulate God's Word in this way. They wrote with the consuming purpose of showing the adopted children ways to move closer to their heavenly Father. They assumed that this would be the force that drove us to the Word of God. It has become, for many, an insurance policy where they are constantly trying to get the best coverage for the lowest premium. How little can I do, how far can I go and still be covered by the Cross?

The reason for the church's very existence demands that its doors be open, in the widest sense of the word, to all who wish to enter, regardless of the attitude of the heart, the person's past mistakes or future intentions. It is only with this willingness that the church of Jesus Christ can minister to those who are hurting and in need of hearing the gospel.

In Matthew 11:28 Jesus makes this open invitation when He says, "Come to Me all you who labor and are heavy laden, and I will give you rest." However, while being open to all, the church must encourage and exhort the process of growth and maturity in its members, and use some criteria to measure that growth and maturity. Sadly, much of the criteria used focuses on the external and not the heart. Usually, the person's physical presence is enough to assure, in the church leaders' eyes, spiritual commitment. If he attends worship service regularly, sings in the choir or joins some type of Bible study, and seems willing to attend and help out at church programs, then his heart is right; he's growing in his faith. Many of our churches are encouraging members to develop a walk based on function rather than an intimate and life–changing relationship with Jesus Christ. If you just play the game of being where you are supposed to be and doing what you are supposed to do, you pass your spiritual maturity test. The membership philosophy comes to be, "Just show me the boundary lines and I'll stay within them." Many times, in getting a spiritual read on a person, the victim will accept the church's criteria instead of God's. "She's always here so she must be all right." Judas was always there also.

Paul, in his letter to the Romans, established what God expects of those who profess Christ and claim the rights and privileges of being adopted into His family: "I beseech you therefore, brethren, by the mercies of God, that you present your bodies a living sacrifice, holy, acceptable to God, which is your reasonable service. And do not be conformed to this world, but be transformed by the renewing of your mind, that you may prove what is that good and acceptable and perfect will of God" (Rom. 12:1–2).

We do not expect everyone to be a perfect and holy living sacrifice; obviously the Romans were struggling with this very issue. It is not where you are, so much as where you are going. If you are headed in the right direction, you can keep yourself from becoming a victim or a chameleon. If you are just sitting beside the road, you will be more available to a chameleon who may wander by.

So before you walk off with just anyone, ask yourself a few questions: Is the person moving toward this goal? Is he searching for the path that will move him closer to being a living sacrifice? Or is he exhausting himself walking a tightrope on the boundary line of the kingdom?

Many times the church has difficulty in distinguishing the difference, but it is not the church that will be required to share a bed, a home, and a life with this person.

A Field Guide to the Spiritual Chameleon

A young man decided to take a trip to Africa. He'd never been to Africa. In fact, he'd never been in any wilderness. A Sunday drive in the country gave his life an adventurous glow. But he was obsessed with the idea of having a great adventure, and the jungles and plains of central Africa seemed to be the ultimate—as adventures go.

He loved to read, so he got all the books on Africa he could find. He got books about geography, climate, native populations, and, naturally, the animals of Africa, especially the dangerous animals. But he had only a short time before he departed and spent most of his time reading about what to buy, where to go, and what to see once he got there. The books on animals would have to wait.

Several months later the young man found himself walking along a jungle path, enjoying his ultimate adventure, when suddenly a ferocious lion jumped onto the path and sat down beside him. Frozen with fear, the young man didn't know what to do. Should he stand there, hoping the lion would eventually leave? Should he make a run for the camp? Or should he make a dash for the nearest tree and wait for help?

When he thought of dashing he felt the weight of his backpack and knew it would slow him down. Suddenly, he remembered what made it so heavy! As the lion sat there and calmly looked at him, he carefully removed the one book he had not had a chance to read—*Dangerous Animals: What To Do When You Meet Them on a Jungle Path.*

As he opened the book, a second lion jumped out from the opposite side of the path and sat down. Now there were two lions, one sitting on his left and the other on his right! With shaking hands and bated breath he began to thumb slowly through the pages looking for the chapter on lions. Finally, thank goodness, he found it. His eyes bulged with terror as he read the first few lines, and, almost simultaneously, both lions leaped on him and ripped the poor fellow apart.

Late that evening the guides from the camp found the young man's mutilated body, and although it was obvious that he had been attacked and killed by lions, they didn't have a clue as to the reason, until one of them found the opened, blood-splattered book on the side of the path. As the two men read the very same lines the young man had read in his last moments, they both nodded in knowing agreement; there in black and white it clearly read, "When finding oneself on a jungle path with a ferocious lion sitting on each side, never, ever read between the lions."

The following guide will give you a quick but accurate look at various species of chameleons: fellowship, financial, romantic, and leadership; information on identification, favorite habitats, feeding habits, and some means of protection. We'll even provide some emergency treatment suggestions should you find yourself in the unenviable position of being a chameleon's victim.

Being concerned, as we are, for your well-being, Jim and I have kept the descriptions of these life cycles brief, so you won't spend too much time "reading between the lions."

THE FELLOWSHIP CHAMELEON

Family: World
Genus: Chameleon
Species: Fellowship

Identifiable Characteristics: The fellowship chameleon has an obsessive need for companionship and social interaction. He has few, if any, close or intimate friends, having little understanding of the dynamics of intimate friendship. He has a willingness to assume spiritual attributes which imply a personal relationship with Jesus Christ in hopes of persuading believers to commit to him as a friend. When the relational and spiritual responsibilities of the friendship begin to demand more than he can give, the fellowship chameleon will move on to other believers in the same body, or to another body of Christ, following the same script.

Habitat: Any Christian body which has a loving concern for new people, a variety of social activities, and a desire to put time and energy into members, that they may grow in their walk with Jesus Christ.

Characteristics of the Victim: Exhibits a strong desire to disciple another believer or establish a strong spiritual friendship. The traits include a fuzzy perspective on the difference between unconditional love and unconditional acceptance and the assumption that everyone in the body of Christ shares a common spiritual experience.

Safeguards: Require those to whom we make ourselves vulnerable and/or commit discipleship time to pass through a spiritual rather than a relational filter.

THE FINANCIAL CHAMELEON

Family: World
Genus: Chameleon
Species: Financial

Identifiable Characteristics: Worships money and other material things. He sees identification as a Christian and relationships within the church as an avenue of financial gain. He considers the body of Christ a viable resource of business contacts and financial transactions. The church reflects honesty and integrity, and he basks in that reflection, giving off a spiritual glow and inviting trust.

The financial chameleon is not only obsessed with his own financial status but usually becomes overly concerned with the church's spending. Because he has no spiritual focus he will see the ministry of the church through a monetary filter—not how many lives are being touched, but how much money is being spent.

Habitat: Prefers either large popular churches with a

significant number of business and community leaders or a small church located in a prosperous part of the community.

Characteristics of the Victim: The victim of the financial chameleon usually has three characteristics that make him or her vulnerable to its camouflage. The first is the assumption that church attendance or membership validates spiritual/financial integrity. The second is that because this person is a Christian they are somehow wiser about the use of money. The third is the victim's own inherent preoccupation with material wealth.

Safeguards: The church of Jesus Christ was not established so that its members could financially "wheel and deal" with one another in some kind of safe spiritual womb that guarantees financial protection and profit. If our interaction with a brother or sister does not have the purpose of causing them to grow in their faith and become more like Jesus Christ, that interaction must be suspect.

If we insist on entering into a financial agreement with a fellow believer, the question must be asked, and honestly answered, "If the worst case scenario took place, and I was financially injured because of this association, would my feelings toward this person remain unchanged?" If you can't honestly answer yes, then you'd better say no to a financial involvement with them.

THE ROMANTIC CHAMELEON

Family: World
Genus: Chameleon
Species: Romantic

Identifiable Characteristics: The romantic chameleon has an obsessive need to possess a person of the opposite sex, relationally and physically. He has few, if any, same-sex friends, especially among Christians. He implies, through casual conversation and shallow involvement in ministry, that he is spiritually focused in order to move romantically into a believer's life.

Habitat: You will find the romantic chameleon in any church or Christian organization having a singles' group. He prefers a church where the pastoral staff and/or lay leadership provide little accountability and shy away from confrontation.

Characteristics of the Victim: The romantic chameleon dines on the widowed, divorced, or never-married people of the opposite sex, with sometimes even the recently separated person as an appetizing possibility. He may actually prefer the divorced person. The dissolution of the marriage has created such devastation to the person's feeling of self-worth that she becomes very susceptible to the chameleon's spiritual camouflage as a loving and caring "Christian" companion. The victim will tend to put her trust in the chameleon instead of a legitimate spiritual authority. He validates her emotionally and relationally with what she wants to hear, sprinkled with just enough spiritual seasoning to be a credible and acceptable authority substitute.

Safeguards: Time and patience are probably the two most effective tools for protecting ourselves from the intrusion of a romantic chameleon into our lives. Before committing to any kind of intimate romantic relationship it is essential that the two people experience a non-physical friendship for at least four to six months. This precaution will allow a variety of circumstances and commitment issues to flow across the friendship, allowing each person to get a better spiritual read on the individual with whom they are considering a romantic attachment.

THE LEADERSHIP CHAMELEON

Family: World
Genus: Chameleon
Species: Leadership

Identifiable Characteristics: His security and self-worth come from the need to be in control of people, projects, and organizations. He is a very functional individual and adept at getting things accomplished. He will see the church as one more organization in which he can enjoy the power of authority. He is not afraid of making decisions and can live with the consequences of being wrong. He will establish and use a spiritual personality to move into positions of authority within the church structure. He does not like to be under others' authority, and if he cannot establish some type of control within a reasonable length of time, he will leave the church.

Habitat: The leadership chameleon can be found in a variety of church environments. He is quickly accepted into churches where programs are more important than people, where the church itself tends to be a functional institution rather than a relational institution. He may also be found in churches that are very relational, especially within the upper staff, and need functional people to establish goals and programs for the church, or simply where there is a weary pastoral staff willing to let someone, anyone, pick up some of the burden, with very little spiritual sifting in the person's life.

Characteristics of the Victim: Believers who value and are impressed by secular, functional abilities and the willingness to make tough decisions, in place of spiritual maturity, love for the body, patience, and a servant's heart.

Safeguards: Before members of the body are allowed to step into positions of authority the church should sift them through various programs and ministries to test them. No one ever appears rebellious when they are always allowed to do what they want to do. See how they respond under others' authority in tasks and circumstances that have little glamour or excitement. It is important to test the servant's heart before establishing a leader's authority.

As you have moved through these classifications it may seem that some of these chameleons would be easily identified by a mature Christian with good spiritual discernment. The problem is that many times we have spiritual blind spots, even those of us who have a close relationship with the Lord and are sensitive to His leading. These blind spots usually come in the form of erroneous belief systems. I do not mean a belief system in the doctrinal sense, but in the sense of our perception of the body of Christ and our ex-pectations of those who make up the body. What are those blind spots, those spiritual and rela-tional cracks that allow the chameleon to move into our lives without a bump or ripple of warn-ing?

Filling in the Blank Canvas

After having read the belief systems of the various species of chameleon and strolled through the classifications of the victims, it may seem like Jim and I have already painted a full canvas, but trust me, the canvas is still nearly blank.

When I was eight or nine years old I loved paint-by-number sets for two reasons. First, I functioned artistically somewhere between a three year old who has just learned that color crayons make pretty marks on paper but really don't taste very good and an expressive orang-utan with a stolen Magic Marker. The paint-by-number set let me pretend that I was a Rembrandt or Michelangelo in the formative years.

The second reason was that I was always amazed at how they turned out. When I first opened up the box and looked at the canvas, with all the squiggly lines representing the myriad of shades and hues that would eventually be trans-formed into a wild stallion standing on a hill, it seemed to me that the company must have definitely made some mistakes; some of the lines and numbers did not fit my perception of what a drawing of a wild stallion should look like. Even as I began to paint I had to keep checking the numbers and colors because I just knew that that particular color in that particular spot was wrong. The painting needed to be almost finished before it acquired any sense of cohesion. Even then, I needed to step back and allow the colors and shades to blend, which made the stallion come alive.

With these first chapters you have opened the box and seen the squiggly lines and numbers of a painting called "The Spiritual Chameleon." There is no color or texture, just a simple outline of an image with a few numbers. At this point you may disagree with my sketch, or wonder if a few of the lines are drawn quite right, or if I might have put a seven where a five should be. In the chapters that follow I will fill in the numbers with bright colors and soft pastels, with shadow and light. I hope that this image I call the Spiritual Chameleon will cease to be just lines and numbers, and will leap off the canvas as a living, breathing creature with needs and appetites that only you, as the victim will satisfy.

PART TWO

CUSTOM COLORS

Chapter 4

THE FELLOWSHIP CHAMELEON

A NASTY SOUND, irritating and persistent, pulled on me until it seemed that, for just a few seconds, I floated between two worlds—that of the warm, womb-like protection of my electric blanket and the unsympathetic reality of a cold, fog–enshrouded morning. The average alarm clock takes its responsibilities much too seriously, and the one I now heard was clearly an over-achiever.

Being the responsible and mature adult my mother raised, I briefly considered getting up at what I foolishly thought was a sensible time. The night before, however, flies had not been frozen to the window, with their pitiful little legs stuck in mid-rub.

I have a definite aversion to frostbite, and mother wasn't there so I reached out and touched the alarm clock with the tender caress of a trash compactor on an aluminum can. Then I snuggled into my favorite fetal position and drifted back into the meandering of an uncluttered mind.

On that cold Saturday morning the bed won simply because it felt better than anywhere else I could imagine. I had a place where I was comfortable and safe from the chilled air, the cold floor, and whatever else might be lying in wait outside that toasty interior. I was willing to rationalize almost anything to remain where I was.

Like that Saturday morning, the world can be a harsh and cold place; friendships can be shallow, commitments based on the convenience of the moment. Many people spend their lives bouncing off friends, relationships, and work associates like a steel ball in a pinball game. Insecurity, unfulfilled expectations, and rejection move these people erratically through a social vacuum until they ricochet into the body of Christ.

A sense of belonging comes from being adopted into the family of God, becoming a child of the King. For many people, coming into the body of Christ is like sliding into a warm bed on a cold night and waking to find that they don't really belong there, but it's just too comfortable to leave. They like the family atmosphere but don't want to go through the adoption process. They understand—if the church is preaching the Word of God—that to be adopted into this family means giving your life away, and that's a big price to pay for a little warmth and acceptance. It's much easier to walk down the aisle and pretend. This is how the fellowship chameleon is born.

The Power of a Spiritual Friend

The fellowship chameleon is probably the least harmful to individuals or to the body as a whole. Their impact on the ministry is rather passive, and people who have been victimized seldom realize it. The fellowship chameleon steals from people's time, prayer life, and ministry motivation in the guise of friendship without their realizing the theft has been made. To understand the fellowship chameleon I believe we must first understand the need that drives him, that is, the strange, elusive, and wonderful creature called friendship.

Friendship is somewhat like nuclear energy. Both are immensely powerful forces having the capacity to change our lives forever. Therefore, they hold a certain fascination for us. We love to read beautiful poems about the emotional power of friendship or see touching movies that portray the sacrifice of friendship. We envy the friendships in the Bible, such as David and Jonathan: "The soul of Jonathan was knit to the soul of David, and Jonathan loved him as his own soul"

(1 Sam. 18:1*b*). Most of us, however, have been touched by that kind of friendship about as often as we have witnessed the launch of a nuclear missile. The power of a close friend fascinates us, but not enough to unleash its power in our own lives.

When I was in high school I remember seeing a film on nuclear energy. In the film scientists were demonstrating how the energy given off by the splitting of one atom causes a chain reaction resulting in an atomic explosion. On a gym floor they had set a thousand mousetraps, each with a ping-pong ball resting on the wire hinge. When one trap was sprung the ball arched into the air, landing on another trap and sending another ball into the air along with the original. Each ball came down on two more traps with the same effect. Within seconds there were close to a thousand ping-pong balls careening off each other in a dance of energy.

Many times in the arena of friendships we put a little energy into it, set off a few mousetraps, and think we have produced the relational equivalent of nuclear fission—the intimate friend.

Casual friendships, on the other hand, make up the majority of the relational bridges we have in our lives and require few mousetraps and very little energy. They often originate in a serendipitous fashion when people fall into our lives filtered by common interests, such as jobs or recreational activities. You might both work in the same office, belong to the same model airplane club, or be in the same class in school. If the common interest is removed, the vacuum that is left usually causes the bridge to crumble.

We don't expect casual friendships to carry much emotional weight. They exist to entertain us like a good book or favorite television show would. If we call and they're having some kind of serious personal problem, we express our sympathy and promise to call back at a better time. Then we take a quick run through the television guide to see what else might fill the evening.

There is nothing wrong with having casual friends. They are comfortable and necessary. They fill gaps in our lives and are the stepping–stones to more meaningful friendships. Close friends typically begin somewhere in the cobweb of time as casual friends. Casual friendships become a problem when they substitute for deeper levels of commitment. For a blind man three shades of gray may constitute a rainbow. For many of us who have no concept of intimate friendship, a casual friend becomes, by default, an intimate friend.

When a fellowship chameleon steps into a body of believers looking for friendship it is usually the relaxed, informal relationship he is seeking. Close, meaningful friends have been outside his realm of experience, so he doesn't know how to develop them or what to look for. If Dorothy hadn't known about the Wizard of Oz, she probably would not have started down the yellow brick road.

Ironically, nonchalant fellowship is not fostered by membership in the body of Christ. In 1 Corinthians 12:24*b*–26 Paul says, "But God composed the body, having given greater honor to that part which lacks it, that there should be no schism in the body, but that the members should have the same care for one another. And if one member suffers, all the members suffer with it; or if one member is honored, all the members rejoice with it." There is nothing casual about suffering and rejoicing with another.

Within the church, social strangers are spiritual friends. The dimension of Christ in our lives gives us a common experience that allows us to touch spirit to spirit, discarding the required social familiarity like so much social trivia. The fellowship chameleon, however, does not want or even understand what is available to him within the unique atmosphere of God's adopted family. He just wants to be entertained, to enjoy companionship, while loving Christians serve his needs.

During a college/career class on relationships I taught, a young woman asked if she might speak with me after the class. As she sat there I sensed she was struggling, so I suggested that we pray. I prayed that her spirit would speak to mine, and that we might feel a oneness in the Lord Jesus Christ. After the prayer she began sharing the heart of an eighteen year old who had never known love in any kind of relationship, having been abandoned by her mother and sexually abused by her father. She had searched for love and finally found it in the person of Jesus Christ.

Those who know me sometimes suggest that I have the sensitivity of a hibernating toad, but that night my heart ached with her pain and leapt within me when she shared her testimony.

We have a fairly large church, and since that class our paths have not crossed that often. But I continue to pray for her and have felt tremendous joy and satisfaction in seeing her grow and become established in God's love. For an hour we had been intimate friends in Jesus Christ. The further away the chameleon moves from intimacy with Christ, the further away he moves from understanding and experiencing that spontaneous supernatural intimacy with fellow believers.

It has been said that the ministry of Jesus Christ is run by tired men. I don't believe that ministering to excited, growing Christians makes one tired; on the contrary, I believe it refreshes and stimulates. It is those who stubbornly refuse to grow, or have no concept of what growth is, who suck the spiritual life out of a leader.

Growth is not some abstract, immeasurable term. It is a process by which a believer's life is conformed to the life of Jesus Christ. The changes can manifest themselves in a myriad of ways, and the only change initially is the willingness to change, an awareness that there is a need for change. Growth is an attitude of gratitude that wells up from the heart and spills over into the lives of others. It arises out of knowledge of the remarkable work God has done for us through His Son. Out of that gratitude comes a willingness to open your life to the sifting of the Holy Spirit through Scripture, prayer, and the input of other believers, that your life might be pleasing to the One who gives the gift, a gift with no payment required or expected; but you realize what joy there is when you acknowledge your gratitude. That thankfulness will be evident in your desire to reach out to other people that they might have the same gift. There is a yearning to invest in others' lives, because God thought you so special that He was willing to invest the life of His Son in yours.

The change may be evident in the simple act of greeting a new person before the worship service and making them feel welcome. It may be an openness toward sharing what Jesus Christ has done in your life with a person by whom you've always been intimidated. The change seems most evident when the believer moves in a direction different from what has been natural for them, when they step outside their comfort zone, not for their own sake but for Christ's. The more often these choices are made the more the cauldron of evidence boils with the statement of change.

Taking a Look at Sam

"These last couple of weeks have been great," said Sam. "Everyone has been so nice and made me feel so accepted that I knew I wanted to be a part of this group. The people where I work just don't seem to understand me. I think a lot of it has to do with my being a Christian. You know as well as I do that spiritual things tend to make unbelievers uncomfortable."

Sam and I were sitting in a small counseling room after the evening service in which Sam had come forward to join the church. For membership in our church it is very important to confirm that the person publicly confesses Christ as his Lord and Savior. As a prayer room counselor I had spent the last fifteen minutes talking with Sam about his conversion experience as a teenager and verifying that he had been baptized. He seemed to enjoy sharing his testimony and responded to all of my questions with the appropriate answers.

He added, "I really enjoyed the youth group at my first church, but since then I haven't been able to find a place where I've felt comfortable. Over the last four or five years I've tried several churches, but I've really been impressed with the people I've met here."

During the next several months Sam and I met regularly for coffee to get better acquainted. He seemed to be doing well in the singles' group and was attending most of the activities. He had signed up for a home Bible study, had volunteered to help out with our evening program, and was thinking about joining the choir. He said he loved to sing and wondered if the singles ever did any skits or presentations? He'd had some drama experience in high school and would be glad to help.

"Sam," I said, "I am very encouraged. You have an enthusiastic spirit and are making a real effort to be part of our family here. I hope your personal relationship with the Lord is doing as well."

"Oh, it is, Terry," Sam replied. "My quiet times and prayer life are so much better since I came here."

"How are they better?" I asked.

Sam paused for a few seconds, a puzzled expression on his face, then replied in a more cautious tone, "Well, you know, better . . . more intense, more emotional . . . just better. Besides, quiet times are kind of private for me, and it's difficult for me to share about them, but I love to share about the Lord!"

"I understand," I said, "I just want to caution you not to get so involved with church programs that you forget to spend time with Jesus."

"Oh, I know what you mean; if it weren't for the Lord none of these other things would be possible."

After almost a year Sam was still with us.

He had been a faithful member of the choir but had dropped out of his Bible study because he thought it was a bit shallow. For a couple of months he helped with the monthly men's night; then, for almost six months, he served faithfully on our evening program committee and participated in several skits and drama productions.

Our evening programs coordinator was getting married and the job would be open soon. Sam came to me one evening after the service and asked if he might be considered for the position.

"Sam," I said, "we've appreciated your help with the evening program this past year, but we expect more of our major ministry coordinators than good programs. They should demonstrate an excitement about sharing their faith and discipling others. There are some areas of your life I'm kind of concerned about. We've encouraged you to take the evangelism class but you're always too busy. I've invited you to an early morning men's study, but you don't seem interested. You've been a Christian a long time, but I don't see you putting time into anyone else. I think there needs to be a change in your spiritual attitude before you can step into this position."

With a short pause and some apparent soul-searching Sam finally said, "Terry, you're absolutely right. I've allowed my walk to become too focused on serving and not enough on growing in Him. I want to thank you for sharing this with me, and I'll do my best to get things turned around."

A year after that conversation Sam was still on the program committee, still in choir, and had one of the best attendance records for social functions in the group. However, he had yet to take an evangelism class, had not brought anyone to church, nor allowed anyone else into the privacy of his spiritual life. What was Sam's prayer life and quiet time like? How was God changing how he viewed himself and those around him? What things was he struggling with, and why, after more than a year in the body of Christ, had Sam not reached out to anyone else? He was pleasant to be around and in many areas of ministry did a lot of work, but Sam was a thief and one of his victims was Don.

Taking a Look at Don

On a typical Sunday we have between 180 and 200 people in our singles' Sunday school. Our group is comprised mostly of adults between the ages of 23 and 59, who are unmarried, separated, divorced, or widowed. If the church were a hospital this would be the intensive care unit where everyone was recovering from open heart surgery.

Don was in charge of the Friday men's night, which met once a month for a variety of activities, from guest speakers to softball games. Many of these men were new Christians, some who had not made a commitment to Christ, but all of them had one thing in common—their lives had been ripped apart by the loss of their wives and they were hurting. The men's night provided a place for them to bond, not only with each other, but with the leadership as well.

Several months after Sam had completed the new members' classes, he joined the men's Friday night committee to help with set-up and be another person for new people to talk with. We encourage our leaders to spend personal time with the people under them, so Don began to meet with Sam once a week. After a couple of months Don and I were discussing the ministry and Sam's name came up. I asked how he was doing.

Don's eyes lit up as he said, "He's doing great! He's got a real servant's heart and helps out with everything. He's a little shy around people, but I think that will improve with time. He seems to have a lot of potential."

"How's your one-on-one time with him? Is he opening up a little bit?"

"He's not quite as mature in the Lord as he implied, and he has some trouble talking about his relationship with Christ, but that could be because he doesn't know me very well. I'm trying to spend more social time with him so he's more comfortable around me, and I'm encouraging him to spend time with some of the new guys." About a month later Don called me at home one evening.

"Terry, I have some concerns about Sam I need to run by you."

"What's the problem?" I asked.

"Well," Don continued, "I'm a little frustrated with Sam. I can't seem to get him moving spiritually. The time I spend with him each Wednesday morning is, quite frankly, kind of boring. He talks about some of the struggles he's having at work with his boss and co-workers, how he enjoys the ministry activities, but not much about how God is moving in his life. He talks a lot about wanting to share with people, but I don't believe he ever has. I don't know of anyone he's brought to church or singles', and his relationships with the people at work don't seem to be changing. I've encouraged him to get into an evangelism class to learn how to share his faith, but he always seems to have a reason or excuse not to."

Don paused for a minute, then continued in a softer voice, "Terry, I'm beginning to wonder if he really knows Christ as his Savior. I haven't seen any kind of change in his life, and I'm getting tired of looking."

I suggested that Don set some criteria for his continued personal time with Sam, one condition being that Sam sign up for an evangelism class. If Sam found a reason not to, then Don should step back in terms of personal time invested in him.

For the past several months Don had put

many hours of concentrated, one-on-one time with Sam, meeting for an hour each Wednesday morning. He had met with him for planning sessions for the men's nights, spent recreational time with him, prayed for him, encouraged him, exhorted him, and finally confronted him. Not counting the physical time Don had invested in Sam there were nearly two months of concentrated emotional and spiritual effort that Don had given to him. Still, he had not been able to touch Sam's heart intimately—unlike that young girl who had touched my heart in less than two hours.

Don had invested himself in Sam because he had assumed that there would be a return on his investment; that what he had given Sam in the name of Jesus Christ, Sam would give to others eventually. Sam had taken what Don had to give, not for the sake of Jesus Christ, but for the sake of casual friendship. Sam had defrauded Don emotionally and spiritually. The fraud was committed not because Sam wanted a friend, but because he had agreed to a discipleship program with no intention of growing in Christ—because he sought only companionship.

Many people see the church as another social club—like the Elks or the Lion's Club—that does good work in the community, has a sense of moral and ethical values, and provides companionship for those of like interests and common goals. Too many people step into a relationship with Christ and His church with a casual attitude, and when they find their needs unfulfilled they just go somewhere else. Although the church provides companionship and friendship in union with Christ that is not its purpose. In Ephesians 2:19–22 Paul says, referring to the church, "So then you are no longer strangers and aliens, but you are fellow citizens with the saints, and are of God's household, having been built upon the foundation of the apostles and prophets, Christ Jesus Himself being the corner stone, in whom the whole building, being fitted together is growing into a holy temple in the Lord; in whom you also are being built together into a dwelling of God in the Spirit" (NAS).

The apostle Peter, speaking to those who have accepted Christ as their Lord and Savior, says, "[Y]ou also, as living stones, are being built up a spiritual house, a holy priesthood, to offer up spiritual sacrifices acceptable to God through Jesus Christ" (1 Pet. 2:5).

Christ did not come to make bad people good, but to make dead people live. We, as part of the body of Christ, are in the business of life and death. For believers who comprehend how serious their obligation is to a lost world, and how few of us there are, and how short the time is, the way we use our time and energy is vital.

My next door neighbor, Ramon, is a fireman. One afternoon I asked him about his job and how he liked it. He couldn't begin to describe the excitement and joy he felt when he was able to help save someone's home—even their life. But one of his most frustrating experiences was being called out on false alarms. Ramon said that several times during his career someone with a genuine emergency suffered because he and his crew were answering a false call.

Christ said to His disciples, "The harvest truly is great, but the laborers are few; therefore pray the Lord of the harvest to send out laborers into His harvest" (Luke 10:2). He is imploring His disciples to pray for workers who will share and disciple, not just develop friendships. There are multitudes who are willing to do more than just accept the gift of salvation, people who are willing to become "laborers" for the cause of Christ. It is these people to whom we owe our time and energy. While Don was pouring what little time he had into Sam there may have been someone who was desperately seeking the influence of a mature Christian in their lives, that they might further the cause of Christ, but Sam had Don answering a false alarm.

It needs to be said that this was not necessarily Sam's fault. Sam was not maliciously pulling a spiritual fire alarm just to get Don's attention, but the result was the same. After someone like Don has gone through two or three Sams the joy of sharing and building into the body of Christ starts fading, because the excitement of being a Christian emanates from seeing change and growth in the lives of those to whom we commit ourselves.

In Philippians 2:1–2 Paul speaks of the source of the joy and encouragement that sustains the worker in his labor: "Therefore if there is any consolation in Christ, if any comfort of love, if any fellowship of the Spirit, if any affection and mercy, fulfill my joy by being like-minded, having the same love, being of one accord, of one mind." When individuals attach to the body of Christ with a different purpose, they can drain the life-blood from a ministry.

A good friend of mine had served for a year in a leprosarium in Africa as a physiotherapist. When she got back to America she shared with me the misconceptions about leprosy. I had always assumed, for example, that the extremities simply rotted away and fell off over a period of time, and that this was inherent in the nature of the disease. Susan explained that what really happens is that the victim loses all feeling in the fingers and toes. When the extremities are injured in some way, the person is unaware of the injury because they have lost all sense of pain and continue to use the in-jured finger or toe. The wound becomes infected and the flesh of the infected skin simply wears away.

The fellowship chameleon works on the body of Christ much like leprosy works on the human body. He first creates a numbness through the camouflage of invented spiritual needs. Once the sensitivity to deceit is removed the chameleon begins to inflict injury to the body by wearing away its time and energy, and its commitment to others. Like Don, one day we find ourselves weary and wonder that we did not feel the erosion of our joy until so much of it was gone.

Our protection lies in our approach to the new person coming into the group. Most of the time we come at people relationally and not spiritually. After spending several hours with them we come to think of how friendly they are, their sense of humor. Are they a good conversationalist? We judge their spirituality through relational issues: If they are a nice person, we tell ourselves, they must have a fairly good spiritual stance. If their conversation is pleasing and they ask all the right questions they must have a genuine interest in me, as a brother or sister in Christ should. We drop the spiritual shield of steel that God has given for protection—consisting of His Word and the Holy Spirit—and pick up a relational shield that the world gives us, made of cardboard.

It is important to connect relationally with people, to be an enjoyable and comfortable person to be around. It's important that people feel that you care about them other than just as a servant in the body of Christ. For people dedicating time to discipling someone, or for that new Christian who is seeking authentic Christian friendship, the person who is the object of your consideration must come through a spiritual grid.

With the other chameleons, their impact on the victim's life cuts through that life with such painful consequences that the victim, if not the ministry itself, becomes more sensitive and alert in preventing that type of exploitation again. The fellowship chameleon, however, moves in and out of a group barely making ripples on the surface, and that's what makes him so pernicious. When the fellowship chameleon is finished with us we wave good-bye and wonder what more we could have done to help him spiritually, when we gave him a gift that was more than he warranted, and more extravagant than we could afford.

Chapter 5

THE FINANCIAL CHAMELEON: Using Jesus Christ as Collateral

A LUNATIC SAT in his cell playing solitaire. His cellmate was watching, and finally spoke up.

"Wait a minute," he cried, "I've caught you cheating yourself!"

The first man placed a finger to his lips. "Shhh, don't tell anybody, but for years I've been cheating myself at solitaire."

"You don't say," said his amazed pal. "Don't you ever catch yourself?"

The first one shook his head. "Naw," he replied proudly, "I'm too clever."

For many of us our financial relationship with the Lord is a lot like the individual who was cheating himself and too clever to get caught. We take whatever amount of money the Lord has given us, whether it be a weekly check, profit from a business transaction, or a sales commission, and we begin to play with it. Like the lunatic, we understand the rules. We know how God feels about that money when Jesus says, "But lay up for yourselves treasures in heaven, where neither moth nor rust destroys and where thieves do not break in and steal. For where your treasure is, there your heart will be also" (Matt. 6:20,21). Notice He does not say where your heart is that's where your treasure will be. In other words, what we place the most value upon is where our heart will be focused.

If we consider the spiritual side of our lives our treasure, then our mind, emotions, imagination, and energy will be focused in that direction. If, however, money is our treasure, then all of those things just listed will be focused upon making money. We say to God: "You didn't deal me the hand I wanted, so I need to move a few of these cards around so I have a better chance of winning, of coming out on top financially, of being a success." Thus the sleight of hand begins.

We think the best way to fool God is to rename our cards so that He won't recognize them. That way we can hold onto the cards a little longer, get more of what we want, eventually getting around to giving Him a share of what we think He should have. God is a little slow in the area of economic terminology, we tell ourselves. We can simply disguise our money with terms like gross and net, capital gains, dividends, deferred interest, IRA's, annuities, and He'll never miss that offering. It's lucky for us that God doesn't have a financial planning consultant or we would probably not be able to fool Him; we would be expected to approach the issue of money as did the Macedonians:

"And now, brothers, we want you to know about the grace that God has given the Macedonian churches. Out of the most severe trial, their overflowing joy and their extreme poverty welled up in rich generosity. For I testify that they gave as much as they were able, and even beyond their ability. Entirely on their own, they urgently pleaded with us for the privilege of sharing in this service to the saints. And they did not do as we expected, but they gave themselves first to the Lord and then to us in keeping with God's will" (2 Cor. 8:1–5, NIV).

If you dressed in camouflage clothing and stood in front of a white wall, chances are you would be seen quite easily. If you crouched down in a thick forest setting, in a multitude of trees, plants, leaves, and colors, you would be difficult to recognize. We get all dressed up in our camouflage terminology and crouch down in the complexities of the modern monetary world. There we can hide our financial attitude and sleight-of-hand from God and from those who might be concerned if they knew. God sees us dressed up in our ridiculous garb, crouched down before the white wall of the Macedonians' example.

We never fool God with these games. We usually do a pretty good job of confusing ourselves, and one who is confused or ambivalent about a thing can easily become a victim. Into this maze of alien terminology steps the financial chameleon who says, "Here, let me help you sort out your cards, these confusing financial concepts; have I got a deal for you!"

The major stumbling block when it comes to the movement of money from one person to another is the issue of trust. Seldom will one person part with money where trust is not an integral part of the transaction. Trust is the offspring of truth and honesty.

In the world it takes years to establish a reputation for financial integrity, but a simple mixture of one part church membership and several parts spiritual pretense yields instant integrity, not only for the business executive seeking investment capital, but for the young couple starting their own business; the local distributor of cleaning products; a church member who happens to be a professional investment counselor.

Lisa was attending our evangelism class. The members of the class called on people who had visited the church, or in some way expressed an interest in spiritual things. After several months the teacher had a chance to sit and talk with an older woman Lisa had brought to Christ through one of the class visits. The teacher asked her if she was excited about her new life in Christ and the woman said of course, and that since she had met Lisa a lot of exciting things were happening in her life.

After further conversation the teacher learned that, after sharing Christ, Lisa had also shared about a new door-to-door cosmetics sales venture she was involved in and recruited her as a sales representative. In addition, Lisa spent most of the one-on-one time discussing sales techniques, not in Bible study as the teacher was led to believe. It was discovered that each time Lisa made a call she also made a sales pitch and was doing quite well.

After being confronted with the problem and asked to stop, Lisa decided that our church was too legalistic and controlling, and decided to attend elsewhere.

When we abuse our relationships with fellow believers in order to achieve financial gain, we risk great damage to the body, especially to new believers. In Matthew 18:6–7 Christ gives a chilling warning: "But whoever causes one of these little ones who believe in Me to stumble, it is better for him that a heavy millstone be hung around his neck, and that he be drowned in the depth of the sea. Woe to the world because of its stumbling blocks! For it is inevitable that stumbling blocks come; but woe to that man through whom the stumbling block comes!" (NAS).

Most Christians in the business community are sincere believers growing in their faith and walking with the Lord, and would never knowingly compromise their faith or their relationship with Christ for financial gain. For some, however, the church is just another relational line in a multitude of lines they have floating in the community.

Because the chameleon lacks spiritual discernment in his life, he lacks integrity and judgment in his business relationships. He compartmentalizes areas of his life and keeps business separate from God. The fact that he is a Christian has nothing to do with how he makes a deal—it's just business. Because the image of this person is framed by a church building some established defenses are ignored.

Walter had just moved into the community and started a new business. He was struggling desperately to get a client base started. One day while at his neighbor's house, Walter noticed a large directory on the dining room table. It was the church directory of more than two thousand members, representing a fairly affluent segment of the community. Walter asked how he might get one and was told that all he had to do was join and one would be sent to him automatically. In this particular church the issue of salvation was not discussed with prospective members. If you wanted to become a member, you were obviously a Christian. Walter had his membership certificate —and his future client base—within a week.

The victims of the financial chameleon usually have three characteristics that make them vulnerable to the chameleon's camouflage. First there is the assumption that church membership/ attendance validates integrity. This common thread runs through each of the chameleon scenarios. We need to remember that there can be a hundred wrong reasons for church affiliation, from joining because of family tradition, to liking the steeple or the sound of the bell. But there are few right reasons, among them being that the Word of God is proclaimed, and your walk with Christ and your faith are nurtured. If it is not for the few right reasons, then spiritual and financial integrity are guaranteed only as much as they are in any secular club.

The second trait of the victim stems from the assumption that Christian business executives will be spiritually wiser about the use of money; that is, they will invest money in ways that they believe honor God.

The world has always been fascinated with money. The human population has spent vast amounts of time, effort, and wisdom on plans and schemes to corner the market on money, and many have been very successful.

God, however, does not seem to care that we become wealthy. In fact, in Proverbs 23:4–5 He says, "Do not weary yourself to gain wealth,/

Cease from your consideration of it./ When you set your eyes on it, it is gone./ For wealth certainly makes itself wings,/ Like an eagle that flies toward the heavens" (NAS). In Matthew 16:26 Jesus asks this question: "For what will a man be profited, if he gains the whole world, and forfeits his soul? Or what will a man give in exchange for his soul?" (NAS). The world, not God, is known for its drive to make and spend money. Thus I believe we need to question fellow believers whose primary concern is the same as the world's.

The world's expertise on the acquisition of money attracts many Christians who would never contemplate seeking secular counsel for emotional or relational issues; without a moment's hesitation, they seek secular counsel in monetary areas. This does not mean that secular financial counselors lack integrity, but they have no spiritual discernment of how God expects His children to handle money. Even believers who serve as financial counselors must be able to separate the spiritual and financial areas of their lives. There is a significant difference between a counselor who happens to be a Christian and a Christian counselor.

The young couple had been married two years and their first child was on the way. The young husband was doing well on his job and had received a promotion. They were both Christians, tithed regularly, and were putting money aside each month in a savings account. After Sunday school one afternoon an older man, who had been a longtime member of the church, approached them. He said he was a professional financial counselor and was wondering if they had planned financially for the future. When they explained what they were doing, he said that he thought they could do a little better and suggested they make an appointment with him.

After talking it over they decided that they probably could use some help, and would much prefer to use a financial counselor who was a Christian, than trust a stranger who was not a believer. After meeting with this man—who was very nice, and seemed open and honest—several investments were suggested and a financial plan was born.

Several months passed. The couple received a packet describing the various investments that had been made and where their money was going. All three of the companies they had invested in were owned by a large tobacco company, which also owned a beer company. Although they were not sure about these particular companies, they were aware that many of the tobacco companies had aligned themselves with the civil liberties organization to fight the ban against smoking, and in so doing had become partners in the support of abortion rights.

When the couple met with their financial consultant and asked him if he realized where their money was really going, he expressed surprise at their reaction. He not only defended the investments as being sound, but said he had steered several other Christian clients in the same direction and would do so in the future. He explained that he really had no alternative but to recommend these companies since they were doing so well; after all, they were in the business of making money, and his employer would have little patience with an investment counselor who did not recommend those types of investments.

Here was a believer who was using the body of Christ as a client resource pool, needing to say little about his spiritual trustworthiness; framed against the backdrop of the body of Christ, that was assumed. Anytime we approach people in a spiritual environment with the intention of personal monetary gain, we are—knowingly or unknowingly—using that environment as an access code to establish trust. I believe he was an honest man and was doing the best he could in giving them sound investment counsel, but he based his counsel upon secular wisdom and discernment. His wisdom came not from God but from his employer, who had absolutely no spiritual discernment and whose only concern was to make money for his clients and himself.

First Corinthians 3:18–20 says, "Let no one deceive himself. If anyone among you seems to be wise in this age, let him become a fool that he may become wise. For the wisdom of this world is foolishness with God. For it is written, 'He catches the wise in their own craftiness'; and again, 'The LORD knows the thoughts of the wise, that they are futile.' "

For the investment counselor to do what was right before God would have seemed utterly foolish to his employer. When the young couple turned down a legal investment that would guarantee a good profit, they probably seemed foolish to the counselor himself.

Though a sincere Christian, this man was looking at the world through a financial filter, not a spiritual filter. He was not looking through the eyes of Christ, but through the world's fascination and hunger for profit. The need for financial gain had made him use his association with the body of Christ to satisfy this need. The condition of his heart and the priorities of his life became clear as he continued to insist that there was no problem.

Matthew 15:14 says, "Let them alone. They are blind leaders of the blind. And if the blind leads the blind, both will fall into a ditch." This man was blind because he was no longer functioning with the wisdom of God, but with the wisdom of the world; thankfully, those he was attempting to lead were not.

Can we assume that God automatically blesses any investment a believer makes? Certainly verses like Romans 8:28 apply to our financial investments, don't they? "And we know that all things work together for good to those who love God, to those who are the called according to

His purpose." Before we assume that God provides Christians with some kind of spiritual insurance policy, we need to consider the possibility that God's definition of good may be different from ours. God may want to give us a kind of good that differs from the material good we are seeking. And He may choose some unlikely means to bring it about. For example, He may use financial loss in our lives to bring about good, particularly if we are making haphazard financial decisions. It's amazing how many of those same Christians who file bankruptcy suddenly grow closer to the Lord than they have been in years.

The third characteristic that opens the door for the financial chameleon is the victim's own greed and preoccupation with material things. Writing to Timothy, Paul says, "But those who desire to be rich fall into temptation and a snare, and into many foolish and harmful lusts which drown men in destruction and perdition. For the love of money is a root of all kinds of evil, for which some have strayed from the faith in their greediness, and pierced themselves through with many sorrows" (1 Tim. 6:9–10).

Once we have moved Jesus Christ off the throne of our lives and placed a dollar sign in His place, we become willing victims for the financial chameleon. "And the rest of it he makes into a god,/His carved image./He falls down before it and worships it,/Prays to it and says,/'Deliver me, for you are my god'" (Isa. 44:17).

The church of Jesus Christ was not established so that its members could "wheel and deal" with one another in some kind of safe, spiritual womb that guarantees financial protection and profit. If our interaction with a brother or sister does not have the purpose of causing them to grow in their faith and become more like Jesus Christ, then that interaction must be suspect.

There is the matter of why you were given the privilege of having a personal relationship with God; to what purpose were you called? Paul had some thoughts about this in his letter to the Romans: "I beseech you therefore, brethren, by the mercies of God, that you present your bodies a living sacrifice, holy, acceptable to God, which is your reasonable service. And do not be conformed to this world, but be transformed by the renewing of your mind, that you may prove what is that good and acceptable and perfect will of God" (Rom. 12:1–2).

The renewing of my mind in the area of financial integrity has always been a problem for me. I grew up loving and admiring my father, and still do. He was, however, a dyed–in–the–wool horse trader. We bought and sold horses as if we owned an equestrian flea market. But he didn't limit himself to horses. He traded cars, pickups, trailers, guns, and whatever else would fit into the classified section of the newspaper. Making the deal was fun, and trampling a few ethical daisies while skipping along on the path of profit was never much of a problem. Most of the men he dealt with ran along the same line and expected no less. It was kind of like a bunch of kids deciding to play tackle football with no pads and no referees. It wasn't life, it was a game, and I learned to play it well.

When I became a Christian, my circle of friends and acquaintances began to change, but my ethical outlook on deal-making had not. I knew it was wrong to lie about what might be wrong with that pickup I was trying to sell, but if the buyer wasn't smart enough to ask the right questions, I wasn't about to volunteer any information.

I was pleasantly surprised at the few questions people asked and attributed this to their ignorance and inexperience. While that might have been true in some cases, most of the time, people simply trusted me. Because I was a Christian, other brothers and sisters in Christ considered me trustworthy. Unknown to me, my spiritual colors were helping me win at the game of "Let's Make a Deal."

One day one of my victims, who was a Christian, confronted me about the problems with a truck I had sold him. He shared his surprise that I had kept back information on the truck's flaws. He hadn't thought to ask if anything was wrong; he assumed I was a brother in Christ and would tell him all I knew. I realized two things that day. The first I already knew but had rationalized: I was responsible to tell the truth to those with whom I dealt, regardless of whether I closed a deal or made a profit. The second was more of a revelation: Christians trusted me simply because I was a Christian. Thus I had tremendous power in my fellow believers' lives, and I had to be very careful how I used that power.

Galatians 5:22–23 says, "But the fruit of the Spirit is love, joy, peace, longsuffering, kindness, goodness, faithfulness, gentleness, self-control. Against such there is no law." I may have missed it, but I don't believe making money was in that list. We gauge spiritual power in our lives by the fruit we produce not the money we make.

If we insist on entering into a financial agreement with a fellow believer, then we must ask and honestly answer the question, "If the worst case scenario took place and one of us was financially injured because of this association, would our feelings and ability to minister to one another or to others remain unchanged?" If we cannot honestly answer yes, then we'd better say no to a financial involvement with that person.

Before you enter into a financial agreement with another Christian you may ask, "Does this person really love God? Has he ever shared anything with me of a spiritual nature with the intensity and excitement with which he talked me into this financial opportunity?"

Matthew 6:24 says, "No one can serve two

masters; for either he will hate the one and love the other, or else he will be loyal to the one and despise the other. You cannot serve God and mammon."

Chapter 6

THE ROMANTIC CHAMELEON

OF ALL THE chameleons in the ministry forest one of the most dangerous and cunning is the romantic chameleon. His intent is not just to use the victim but to possess, relationally and physically. The romantic chameleon has the ability to anesthetize the person with the emotional drug of romantic love, and then surgically cut into every area of the victim's life. Unlike the other chameleons who move into our lives, take something from us and move out, the romantic chameleon has the frightening capacity to become one with a believer, temporarily through sexual intimacy, or permanently within the bonds of matrimony.

A little further into the book we will give you what could be considered some unusual—if not downright bizarre—ideas for neutralizing the romantic chameleon's camouflage. Of course, flossing your teeth may seem bizarre until you've experienced a root canal or smelled burning enamel while listening to the high–pitched scream of a drill burrowing into nerve endings. The intensity and consistency with which one flosses is directly related to the number of visits to the dentist for something other than a checkup. The intensity and consistency with which one applies the principles set forth in chapter 8 is proportional to one's experience with romantic chameleons. Before we try to convince you to floss, let's see what a trip to the dentist is like.

The Double-Reverse with a Half-Twist Blessing

Sandra had been in the singles' group for close to a year. When she stepped through the doors of the church, she felt she was worth very little to anyone. Her husband of five years had left her for another woman; she had little education and the end of her marriage seemed like the last in a long succession of failures. The future held even less hope. Then she met Jesus Christ.

She accepted His forgiveness, then gave Him her life, and for the next year He began to heal the wounds that the world had inflicted upon her. By the end of that first year Sandra was beginning to minister to others as she had been ministered to and finding, through that process, that she did have great worth.

Sandra worked as a receptionist for a small sales company and was sharing what God had done for her with her fellow employees. Matt was a salesman for the company, and when Sandra shared her testimony with him and invited him to church he accepted. Matt attended church over the next several months, began coming to the singles' Sunday school class, and sat in on Sandra's Wednesday night Bible study. They began dating, as well as attending church activities together. When challenged about dating a non-Christian Sandra expressed belief that God had brought Matt into her life that she might bring him to Christ. She said she was very encouraged about Matt's attitude and felt sure he was close to accepting Christ as his Savior.

After another month had passed both Sandra's and Matt's attendance began to fall off, and when asked about this they always had a reason or excuse. Finally, Sandra announced that she and Matt were going to be married. When they met with Jim to arrange the ceremony he informed them that he would not marry a believer to a non–believer. Even if Matt were a believer, it was the church's policy that a couple had to attend an eight–week premarital class before they could be married in the church.

At this point Matt became angry, and in a

very blustery tone told Jim that no church or pastor was going to tell him when or where to be married. If this church wasn't going to do it, he could sure find one that would, and with that stomped out of the office. Sandra sat there dazed and confused. What had happened to this loving, sweet man she had known for the past several months?

What had happened was that the chameleon had suddenly had a change in the surface on which he was sitting, a change that he didn't expect, and when the background changed color so quickly, his camouflage couldn't keep up.

In the chapter on "Animal Identification" I said that a chameleon likes a scripted environment, one in which he knows what's coming and has time to change color to match the response that's expected. Sandra had an opportunity to catch a glimpse of the real man instead of the man she thought she was going to marry.

After the meeting in the office that day Sandra had a difficult choice to make and finally made the right one. But having to make that choice was not without a price. Somehow she felt God had tricked her and that the ministry had robbed her of a chance for marital happiness. Her spiritual life was put on hold, and she attended church and Sunday school out of obedience and for the friendships she had made, but little else. Three months later she heard that Matt had married, but it wasn't until almost six months after that that Sandra understood the grace of God.

She was sitting in Sunday school one morning when a young lady sat down at her table. After some conversation the lady shared that she had been separated for several weeks because her husband had been physically abusive to her. She was staying with her parents because she was still frightened of what he might do. She had met the man at another church in town and believed he was a mature Christian. That was why she was not only hurt but shocked at his violent temper and abusive treatment. As they continued talking, Sandra found to her uneasy amazement that the man who had created such physical and emotional terror in this woman's life was the very man who had sat in Jim's office with Sandra less than a year before.

God had surrounded Sandra with a hedge of protection that she had not asked for, was not even aware existed, and at times even resented. The Lord had placed in her life a variety of people with clearer vision and discernment who were able to bring a blessing of protection to her life. I believe Sandra was doubly blessed because she was allowed to see the path her life could have taken had God not protected her. Ephesians 3:20, in the Amplified Bible says, "Now to Him Who by the power that is at work within us, is able to do superabundantly, far over and above all that we [dare] ask or think—infinitely beyond our highest prayers, desires, thoughts, hopes or dreams." It's important to understand that the blessing in Sandra's life came because she did not trust her feelings but trusted God instead, and was obedient regardless of what she wanted to do. The romantic chameleon loves those who leave spiritual discernment, trusted council, and godly obedience in the dust. He preys on those who are obedient to their emotions and spontaneous with their decisions.

Being Taken for a Ride

I once saw a movie where, in order to escape from some danger, a man climbed into a hot air balloon and cut the rope. As he rose into the air a tremendous feeling of relief swept over him as he left the danger behind. Very soon, however, he realized that he had no idea of how to direct the balloon; he didn't know how to land it or even change direction, so for better or worse, he would have to go where the balloon took him—unless, of course, he wanted to jump to his death. He had no idea where the balloon was headed because it was completely at the mercy of the air currents and weather patterns. He finally died of exposure and lack of water, still hoping that the balloon would sink back to earth.

When one stands beside a romantic chameleon and repeats wedding vows it's like stepping into that balloon and cutting the rope. The one thing that distinguishes the life of a Christian is a direction and purpose. The Christian's decision-making process is sifted through prayer, Scripture, counsel, accountability, and the discernment of the Holy Spirit. His choices center around the desire to live in holiness, to grow in Christ, and to bring others to a saving knowledge of Jesus Christ. There is tremendous security in Romans 8:28: "And we know that all things work together for good to those who love God, to those who are the called according to His purpose." This tells us that God has a wonderful plan for our lives, and that through God's guidance we can live an abundant and satisfying life.

When you become attached to a romantic chameleon you soon realize that you have committed yourself to a living lie. You discover that the only plan that was part of your spouse's life was to perpetuate the lie in order to possess your heart. Both of you have been driven by romantic infatuation. As it wears off, the chameleon no longer feels the need to keep up the spiritual charade, and begins to slip back to his pre-spiritual colors. As your infatuation dissipates you get your first clear spiritual look at what you have committed yourself to. It's like finishing a murder mystery: once you know who the killer is you think back through the book, recognize all the obvious clues, and wonder how you could have missed them.

It is especially difficult for a woman who finds herself married to a chameleon, for there is the aspect of spiritual submission to a non-spiritual man. She now finds herself in that relational balloon—the rope having been cut with the wedding vows—and attached to a man for whom Romans 8:28 has no meaning, and therefore no validity; a man with no spiritual direction or discernment, making choices based on self-centered desires, and with priorities established by a world system governed by Satan.

Proverbs 25:19 says, "Confidence in an unfaithful man in time of trouble/Is like a bad tooth and a foot out of joint." She finds herself in a relational balloon whose direction is at the mercy of a man who thinks he can control the winds of the world.

Leading by Default

Married to a chameleon, you will become the spiritual leader regardless of the level of your spiritual maturity. You will find yourself with the wearisome duty of trying to generate spiritual energy in a person who has no intimate knowledge of Jesus Christ. You will become an evangelist and a frustrated discipler with a rebellious congregation of one.

When we witness to friends, relations, coworkers, and others that the Lord brings into our

lives, the act of witnessing has an objective atmosphere in terms of sharing Christ and leaving the
results to God. Whether the person accepts or
rejects Christ is between him and the Lord.

Although we want very much for them to
experience the joy of salvation and the limitless
possibilities of knowing Jesus Christ personally
and are saddened when they reject Him, we can
step away knowing that the consequences of that
decision are on their shoulders and not on ours.

When you marry, however, the Scripture
says you become as one. When you are married to
a chameleon you are intimately tied to that person, and his decisions in terms of Jesus Christ
intensely affect your life. This aspect of oneness
piles tremendous pressure on your marital witness. Your spiritual life begins to vacillate in terms
of how you see your spouse doing, because now
you realize how well he can show you whatever he
wants you to see.

In his book *Too Close, Too Soon* Jim alludes
to the fact that the slower person in a relationship
will control its speed, whether in terms of romance or the spiritual side. No matter how strong
or determined you are as a spiritual partner, the
other will drag on you like a lead weight on a
drowning person. You will finally tire of praying
for the concerns of your life together; tire of going to Sunday school where there are singles and
marrieds, but no ministry for incomplete couples;
tire of seeing your faith and trust in God hinging

more and more on what He is doing—or seems not to be doing—in your spouse's life. Eventually you will tire of even attending church; tire of him going one direction on Sunday and you another. More than anything else, however, you will tire of your inability to share the most important thing in your life with the most important person in your life. For the one person you had looked to for encouragement and a refreshment of spirit is the one person who wearies you beyond comprehension.

The Root of Bitterness

"My soul loathes my life;/I will give free course to my complaint,/I will speak in the bitterness of my soul" (Job 10:1).

If devout Christians, married to chameleons for several years, happened to read this verse describing Job's frustration, I believe their eyes would brim with tears of empathy. Like Job, they would begin to loathe their very lives and speak out in the bitterness of their souls. The feeling of being trapped, condemned to spending the rest of their married lives locked in "rooms of regret" wondering what might have been, will already have begun to beat on their souls.

They will see people in marriages where neither one is a Christian, seemingly more happy and more content than they are. They will wonder, as did Job, why the Lord seems to smile on the wicked. They will believe, as did Job, that the Lord has something against them. They will feel they are being punished for their mates' sins, and that only the Lord can rescue them. But they will feel out of frustration that the Lord's own commandments concerning marriage keep the jaws of their trap closed tightly.

Going Crazy with Love

Ellen had been coming to the singles' class for about three months, and her divorce had been final for about that long. Larry had been with us about six months, had been divorced for two years, but during that time had had several serious relationships outside of the church. He was a brand new Christian while Ellen had grown up in a Christian family and had accepted Christ as a young girl.

Within three weeks of meeting each other, against all counsel from the church, family, and friends, they were married by a justice of the peace. Inside of a year they were divorced, with Ellen back in church trying to put her life together, and Larry lost back into the world.

Eromania is a term often used by our singles' group to describe the amazing process in which a relatively sane person is transformed into one with the emotional and mental stability of a love-sick aardvark. From our observation—and experience—people can become literally "crazy in love." Thus the word *eromania.*

No one residing on planet earth is immune to this malady. It floats across culture, age, and religious beliefs like the smell of hot, rich coffee on a cold frosty morning. Eromania makes "falling" in love fun, and generates an energy and a power that defies human understanding.

The Song of Solomon describes the love and marriage of Solomon to a maiden called the Shulamite. It speaks of the beauty of a pure love between a man and a woman, and how that love can blossom into mutual devotion that becomes supernatural within the sacredness of the marriage vows. It is eromania at its best because it is submissive to God and His plan for both Solomon and the Shulamite woman. It expresses how Christ feels about His bride, the church. Anyone who has experienced eromania, now has an emotional reference to how Christ feels about us.

Even at its best, however, eromania transforms one into an individual that can be difficult to recognize. Listen to how Solomon, the wisest man of his time, spoke of one of the many women in his life: "Behold, you are fair, my love!/ Behold, you are fair!/ You have dove's eyes behind your veil./Your hair is like a flock of goats,/ Going down from Mount Gilead./ Your teeth are like a flock of shorn sheep/Which have come up from the washing, . . . / Your lips are like a strand of scarlet,/ And your mouth is lovely" (Song of Sol. 4:1–2, 3*a*). Solomon continues with these descriptions for three or four more paragraphs and then finishes in verse 7 with, "You are all fair, my love,/ And there is no spot in you."

The man who spoke these words had been selected by God to rule over His chosen people, one of the strongest and most respected nations of that time. Here was a man who was wise enough to ask for wisdom when given the opportunity to have anything he wanted. Rulers from all over the world brought him gifts in exchange for the privilege of hearing the wisdom which God had given him. In Scripture the examples of Solomon's wisdom deal with the relational struggles people had with one another rather than decisions of state. He had a supernatural ability to clear away all of the subjective, emotional turbulence that confrontational issues drag with them, and discern and communicate in a clear way the solutions to the everyday problems his people brought before him.

If the above passage were the only window through which we could view Solomon, I believe we would have difficulty trusting the writer of the above words to make an objective, rational decision about important issues in our lives. This paragon of wisdom suddenly seems to have the emotional mind-set of a high school student who's been mesmerized by the cute blond sitting in front of him in freshman English. Solomon collected a harem of over seven hundred wives and princesses and three hundred concubines. He chose women from among the Hittites, Ammonites, Edomites, Moabites, and Sidonians, and allowed them to practice idolatry and set up pagan shrines in Jerusalem and the surrounding countryside. They became a major factor in Solomon's eventual spiritual ruin.

Like no other process in our sphere of emotional experience, eromania can erase all of the spiritual discernment God has given us, which helps us to screen those who would interact with us on an intimate, romantic level. Eromania has properties which allow this relational surrender to flood our lives without us realizing that the water's rising.

Total Subjectivity, or, Thirty-five Going on Fifteen

When I am not thrashing around writing a book, I teach junior high school for a living. I suppose that's why I appreciate the passage from the Song of Solomon. In class I intercept notes like Solomon's at the rate of two or three a week by people obsessed with getting a driver's license, getting a date, and getting rid of acne—not necessarily in that order. Granted, their notes may not be quite as descriptive or romantically sophisticated, but the heart's motive is synonymous with

Solomon's: the obsession to possess another person relationally.

It matters not how often a person has been through eromania, the next time is always unique; the next person is always different. Past relationships have little validity in producing a wise spirit in a current relationship. If he chooses not to use those past experiences as an operational base, a thirty-five year old can be expected to function with about as much relational wisdom as an adolescent. No matter what our age, the hormones will get into gear. Eromania heightens our awareness of our sexuality at the most inopportune times.

Those thoughts will become hopeful daydreams and fantasies that race ahead of reality, like Secretariat leading the field in the Kentucky Derby. There will be confusion in not understanding exactly how or why you feel the way you do. You will live with anxiety about what to do if the person of your dreams doesn't respond; what if he does? Your life will take up residence on an emotional roller coaster where a simple smile can cause your pulse to race, and the lack of a late night phone call will keep you up till early morning, floundering in a well of melancholy. All who move through the emotional maze of eromania, whether fifteen or sixty-five years old, are kindred spirits.

I am probably one of the most objective people I know. I can take criticisms, challenges, problems, and even people, hold them out at arm's length, turn them around so that I get a view of each side, and make a decision if necessary. The decision is based on information acquired outside of myself and involves little feeling or emotion. I can live with the consequences of those decisions, good or bad.

There is one glaring exception to my objective, almost robotic functioning: my wife Jo Ann. When I interact with Jo Ann my objective nature takes on the consistency of Silly Putty.™

What she says, how she feels, and how she responds to what I do or say, slides down into my well-hidden emotional warehouse. There it opens up boxes labeled delight, dejection, euphoria, discouragement, anxiety, security, and a hundred other blends of feelings reserved especially for her. Not only has God given me a deep love for this woman, but in five years of marriage the eromania has yet to evaporate, for it makes the most objective of us totally subjective with the person to whom we are drawn.

When we are subjective toward another person, everything he or she does and says is taken inside where our thoughts and emotions interpret and give it back many times changed, skewed by our own desires and insecurities.

When I am speaking at a conference I am seldom aware of individuals in the audience, unless Jo Ann is present. If she is there, especially if she is sitting in the front row, much of my attention is focused on her. I read her facial expressions and body language. In this way, I interpret my effectiveness. She may be frowning because she's wondering if she turned the oven off, but because of the way I decode her expression, I conclude that I am blowing a major presentation.

Within marriage, the fragrance of eromania encourages a healthy subjectivity, which creates in husband and wife a servant's attitude toward each other and allows us to enjoy that servant's role. In marriage, healthy eromania is based on what we know about our spouse's strengths and weaknesses. We find joy and excitement in loving them and accepting them, knowing that we are loved and accepted in the same way.

Within a dating relationship, however, there is not the comfort of assumed acceptance that allows this aspect of love to play the role God intended. It's an unhealthy infatuation based upon not what we see but, in many cases, what they keep hidden.

A few years ago a woman in our singles' ministry became involved with a man who was new to the group, but who was a growing Christian, sincere in his faith. After dating him for several months she was ready for marriage, and was not open to any counsel that would impede the relationship.

Ultimately, he shared with her that his first marriage broke apart because of his sexual abuse of his seven-year-old daughter and that, although he was a Christian, he was still struggling with this issue in his life. The reality of who he was and what he was capable of doing quickly evaporated a seemingly rock-solid commitment on the woman's part. Up to that point what lay hidden allowed eromania to trap her in a relational fog, focused on keeping the relationship alive. It was remarkable how objective she became and how clearly she saw what needed to be done once she had all the information.

Eromania thrives on a lack of information —or a certain amount of well–placed misinformation—and so does the relational chameleon.

A New Image of Ourselves

We spend the majority of our lives obsessed with the question "How do I appear to others?" An intimate relationship is the ultimate validation of our worth as individuals. If someone willingly moves into our lives at this level of commitment and intensity, it gives us a sense of meaning and value not only to ourselves, but, we believe, before the world.

We always have "image shapers" in our lives. Our parents, teachers, friends, peers, bosses, and even the media have set criteria for what is acceptable and unacceptable in our behavior, priorities, goals, and relationships. It is the lifelong accumulation of approval or disapproval that determines how we see ourselves and, in turn, establishes how much we feel we are worth to ourselves and to others. In other words, the self-image we accept from the world establishes how much we feel we are worth as an individual. After a person moves through a separation or divorce and has been the one left, he or she suddenly feels worth about as much as last year's fashions, hanging in the bargain basement with a two-for-one tag on the collar.

I am always astonished at the power a new romantic interest has in a person's life. What Jesus Christ has been trying to do for years is accomplished within a few weeks or even days by that special someone. We feel better about ourselves than we have in a long time, and life itself seems somehow cleaner and fresher. Although I hesitate to use the term, it feels almost as if we've been "reborn." We look into the other person's eyes and see a reflection of ourselves that we didn't know existed. We suddenly feel younger and more energetic. We have something to look forward to, and what were fantasies now edge closer to reality. We have not only a new relationship but a new image of ourselves, and we feel like we're part of the new spring line. That is why it is so difficult, even for a believer, to accept counsel that threatens that relationship, for it is the very image we have of ourselves that is at stake.

Novocaine for the Heart

Let's pretend, just for fun, that one Saturday afternoon while driving your brand new sports car down a steep, hairpin mountain road, you had taken one curve too fast, hit the brakes too late and sailed over the edge of a cliff. Let's also pretend, just for fun, that this crash resulted in a multitude of serious injuries and a brush with death itself.

Would you, after being discharged from the hospital and having recovered sufficiently, buy another sports car, take it up to the top of that same mountain and drive down even faster than you did before?

I would hope not. Yet every Sunday we meet people—of both the male and female variety —who live like this. They crawl out of the wreckage of a broken relationship, or the pain of loneliness or feelings of inadequacy, and through the doors of our singles' ministry in search of something that will ease their emotional pain and heal their self-image.

The quickest and most effective way to mask the pain of emotional injuries from a broken relationship is another relationship. Where we once felt rejection, we now feel acceptance; where we once felt unloved, we now feel loved; where there was a sense of being taken for granted we now feel special; where there was anxiety, insecurity, and loneliness, there is now a perceived future of companionship and relational safety. "Don't talk to me about what's going to happen in three months! All I know is that I feel better now than I have in a long time, and don't you dare try to take that away from me!"

When something makes us feel like we are fifteen again, and at the same time effectively masks our pain and fear, we simply close our minds and hearts to counsel that jeopardizes what we are experiencing. It is a scenario custom-made for the romantic chameleon. Very little camouflage is needed to move into the life of one who longs for eromania, or any feeling, to cover the pain he or she may feel. There is little need to change colors when the victim is having trouble simply distinguishing between black and white.

Walking around blind, even with someone leading us, can lead to stubbed toes and bruised knees. But when we refuse to take anyone's hand and start running as fast as we can with our eyes tightly shut, we may very well find ourselves with some injuries that could incapacitate us for the rest of our lives.

Chapter 7

THE LEADERSHIP CHAMELEON:
Make a Decision and We'll Follow You Anywhere!

OF ALL THE chameleons, I believe the leadership chameleon is the scariest because he has the ability to divide the body of Christ.

I heard somewhere that all denominations originated in sin, in the separation of one religious group from another. This splitting or tearing of the body is precipitated by disagreement and/or anger, bitterness, and finally rebellion. In Jesus' High Priestly Prayer, just before His crucifixion, this very concern was expressed to His Father: "I do not pray for these alone, but also for those who will believe in Me through their word; that they all may be one, as You, Father, are in Me, and I in You; that they also may be one in Us, that the world may believe that You sent Me" (John 17:20–21).

Adolf Hitler taught the human race a powerful though tragic lesson about itself: the man who is critical of the status quo will always gather followers. Hitler attained power by focusing on two things: an ongoing, destructive criticism of the government of that time, and by turning the resulting frustration and hatred onto a specific segment of the population—the Jews.

For those who do not have the ability or courage to express criticism or displeasure, they will find an outlet in the man or woman who is willing to listen to their objections and condemnations, and then publicly voice them with more skill, energy, and power than the follower could hope for.

The first concern of Paul in his letter to the Corinthians was this very issue: "Now I plead with you, brethren, by the name of our Lord Jesus Christ, that you all speak the same thing, and that there be no divisions among you, but that you be perfectly joined together in the same mind and in the same judgment. For it has been declared to me concerning you, my brethren, by those of Chloe's household, that there are contentions among you" (1 Cor. 1:10–11). The frustration among the people of Chloe's household made them susceptible to the leadership of a chameleon.

There is something addictive about hearing your own frustration, anger, or bitterness expressed so eloquently, cloaked in spiritual garb, but in Ephesians 5:6 Paul warns us of our responsibility in choosing and following the leaders we do. We see from this verse not only our responsibility but also the consequences of our choices: "Let no one deceive you with empty words, for because of these things the wrath of God comes upon the sons of disobedience."

Time is the enemy of the chameleon. Sooner or later, the leadership chameleon will realize that there is no spiritual base in his life on which he can continue to support a position of authority. The holes and gaps in his life will begin to show through as spiritual challenges and situations flow over him. As the spiritual weaknesses in his life begin to dominate he will try to refocus the attention of the body onto the spiritual weaknesses he perceives in the lives of those over him. As he voices these criticisms he becomes a magnet that attracts the discontented, and a body-within-the-body will develop like a tumor. Just like cancer, the disease is often missed or ignored until the pain is felt, and by then it is too late; it has moved through and infected many parts of the body.

The leadership chameleon is not easily recognized if a church staff is doing what they get paid for, loving and accepting people into the body of Christ. Whether it is a pastor or a lay leader, there is usually a hopeful, optimistic attitude concerning those coming into the fellowship. Along with this hope, there is a built-in radar that picks up vibrations of excitement and intensity, which act as a power source for ministry growth and development.

Many times it is hard for our radar systems to distinguish between the excitement seen in one who has met the Savior and the excitement born out of a drive to control and dominate. Most of the time the staff's image of the person is blurred, simply because we so desire faithful and available people. We love people who are enthusiastic and willing to give of their time and talents. There are so few that when one comes along we pant so hard that our glasses fog up, making it difficult to get a clear picture of the person's commitment and direction.

To look, with a positive attitude, at people, appreciating their potential in Jesus Christ, is by no means a fault; would that more had that response. However, we must not let our enthusiasm for others cause us to leapfrog over the essential question in each person's life: "Do you really know Christ as your personal Lord and Savior, and what is the evidence in your life?" If we allow only external abilities to validate what appears to have happened spiritually, and then based upon that validation give them positions of authority, we may find a future of regret awaits us.

Some leaders are really great. They set the pace and make the tough decisions. We admire their vision, their accomplishments, and we appreciate how nice it is to step in and follow their impetus, riding along on an emotional jet stream. It's exhilarating to be around charismatic leaders; they are where the action is, where the energy is. People are drawn to leaders; Christians are no exception.

The Fight to Survive

I always enjoy what I call the "lifeboat movies," people stranded together, struggling for survival. Maybe their plane crashed on a deserted island; an ocean liner capsized in the middle of the Atlantic; or they might find themselves on the top floor of a burning high-rise. The group faces life–and–death decisions, and someone has to make them.

The issue that fascinates me is that a leader, one who will be given the opportunity to make these decisions, is seldom chosen by the rest of the group. In fact, after the leader mysteriously takes charge, the troublemaker—there is usually a troublemaker in the group—always asks the question, "Who died and made you leader?" To which our fearless leader replies, "Well, someone has to do it," supported by a passive nodding of heads by the rest of the group.

Usually I find myself agreeing with the troublemaker, or at least wondering why this particular character is dressed in a cape with a large red *S* on his chest. Generally, the leader is attractive, has a great smile and has some sense of morals. The question is, am I willing to put my life in the hands of a person just because he's photogenic? The only alternative I see is the troublemaker, with a face that a pitbull would fall in love with.

I'm afraid many of our churches function like those people in the lifeboat movies. A church is usually stranded in the middle of the chaotic and dangerous environment of the world. Many times spiritual life–and–death decisions are necessary, and those very choices can mean the survival or demise of that local group of Christians. When those decisions aren't made, or are made by the wrong people, the consequences can be spiritually devastating.

During the time of the prophet Ezekiel, Israel was a rebellious and obstinate nation with a definite leadership problem. They were so bad that God had already exiled part of them in Babylon, along with Ezekiel himself. While Ezekiel was in Babylon, God spoke through him to those in captivity and to those still free in Palestine. He warned them of the impending destruction of Jerusalem and the enslavement of many more of the Hebrew nation. Several times he placed the problems of His chosen people at the feet of the nation's leaders. In Ezekiel 22:30 God says, "So I sought for a man among them who would make a wall, and stand in the gap before Me on behalf of the land, that I should not destroy it; but I found no one."

In those days, when the nomadic tribes of the desert stopped for the night, they built a hedge of thorns to keep in their herds. It wasn't convenient to build an actual gate, so a man would stand in the gap of the hedge to keep the animals from wandering out and, more importantly, to keep the predators from coming in and attacking the flock. God compared the nation Israel to the flock, saying that no one would build up the wall of faith and commitment. No one would take responsibility for preventing the Hebrew flock from going out, mixing with the Gentiles and their false gods, or for thwarting the Gentiles from coming into the camp of the Hebrews, diluting the Hebrew faith with false worship. He found no one who would step into that leadership role.

Most people, being the intelligent folks that they are, are hesitant to try and fill the gap that will give them that kind of responsibility, so many churches run with a leadership vacuum.

Small churches have the luxury of focusing their leadership on the pastor, and maybe an assistant pastor. As a church grows, however, there are more Sunday school classes, Bible studies, and discipleship groups. Lay leadership takes on a more significant role in the relational part of the ministry, while the pastors begin to operate in the more functional side of the ministry.

A pastor may find himself dealing with the church calendar, Sunday's program, and the up-coming married's conference. The Bible study leader, however, will deal with a young unwed mother in his group, and the Sunday school teacher will answer the scriptural questions of a young man trying to decide on a direction for his life. The church's lay leadership begins to answer many of the body's questions and give direction to those who are trying to survive in a world system geared to destroy them spiritually. As the church grows the lay leadership is stretched, leaving rips and cracks in the leadership fabric. The leadership chameleon slips through these gaps and into positions of spiritual authority.

The driving force behind the leadership chameleon is the obsession to be recognized as a leader. Two types of chameleons emerge out of this obsession with control. They are alike in their need, but are born out of opposite environments.

The Unrequited Leader

It's tough to be a leader in the world; there are rules. Rule one is that leaders must have followers, and rule two is that after following the leader, the follower had better be happy about where he ends up. Success is a definite must for all would-be leaders. The world isn't very forgiving when the leader doesn't meet its expectations; today's leader may be tomorrow's contrite follower.

At times the church gets people who have an unrequited passion to be a leader. People who, for good reasons, have not been allowed a leadership position in the outside world. It's sad to say, but in many churches it is easier to get a lay leadership position than it is to get an assistant managerial position at your local fast–food restaurant. It is an obtuse world, indeed, where the preparation and consumption of a Big Mac is done with greater care than the preparation and consumption of God's Word.

The church provides a perfect environment for those who aspire to leadership. Carried within the essence of the Christian walk is a submissive spirit and a willingness to serve, so rule number one is met: followers are provided at no extra cost. There are immense areas having leadership vacuums in churches today. In our society Christian responsibilities usually trot at the heels of family and career. The attitude of "that's what the pastor gets paid for" leaves many churches begging for leaders, and the old saying that "beggars can't be choosers" is what leaves the door open for the chameleon leader. If he's faithful, dresses well, speaks in complete sentences, and hasn't been arrested in the last year, he may be a candidate for a leadership position. Many times it doesn't require much camouflage to fool us.

Martha had been a widow for several years and was living on her husband's retirement benefits. After his death she had tried to get a job but was qualified for very little. She was aggressive and opinionated, which caused her to be fired from the two jobs she managed to land. When her husband was alive they were nominal churchgoers, attending when it was convenient, and on Christmas and Easter.

Several months after losing her last job Martha found that she had time on her hands and few friends to fill it, so she began attending church more regularly. She made several friends and became involved in the Sunday school class. Because of her personality she was not shy about sharing and had many opinions, regardless of the fact that her spiritual knowledge and experience lacked depth. When she spoke, she spoke with authority and conviction that came not from a close, consistent walk with Jesus, but simply from her personality.

Martha spoke with conviction and authority on subjects ranging from the best way to pick a ripe watermelon to the political issues of the day.

One Sunday morning during the class the teacher shared that they desperately needed a women's Bible study leader for some of the new women in the group. Martha immediately volunteered and, because there was no one else, got the job. She got the job also because we sometimes assume that an authoritative voice and a willingness to speak out is synonymous with spiritual maturity and leadership skills.

The Bible study met once a week and several months passed by with few problems. The pastor asked Martha how things were going; she said just fine. Although some of the women were struggling with some issues in their lives, it was not important enough to concern him. Of course, just because the water is calm doesn't mean there aren't crocodiles in it.

One afternoon a young woman from the group came to see the pastor and broke into tears as soon as she sat down. She and her husband had been struggling in their marriage for several months, basically because her husband was not a Christian and he resented her involvement in the church. She said that up until the week before she had really felt that God wanted her to do everything she could to save her marriage, and bring her husband to the knowledge of Jesus Christ as his Lord and Savior.

The pastor assured her that that was exactly the direction and commitment that God and the church would have her pursue and that he would support her in every way possible.

Confused, she said, "I don't understand. Martha, my Bible study leader, said exactly the opposite—that I needed to divorce this nonbeliever and find myself a 'good Christian man' to marry."

Naturally, Martha got quite a bit of the pastor's attention during the next several weeks. He found that Martha had been giving counsel on a variety of subjects including marital problems, child rearing, and career moves, as well as spiritual matters, not so much from the Word of God, but from the word of Martha. Several of the young women had dropped out of the group because there was doubt in their minds about how the group was being led. When the pastor asked them why they had not spoken to him about these problems, they shared that since he had given her the position, they assumed he supported what was taking place in the study. They felt as though it would be better to drop out than create any problems.

After several personal meetings with Martha, the pastor concluded that Martha did not belong in the position of a Bible study leader, regardless of her personality. Her inexperience was not the only issue, but also her spiritual immaturity, lack of discernment, and ultimately the question of whether she actually had a saving relationship with Christ.

It is hard to measure the damage done to the spiritual growth of the women in that study. How much had she affected their perception and trust in the church? Their willingness to step into ministry at a later date? What image of a spiritual leader had Martha created in their minds? Much if not all of this could have been avoided had those meetings taken place before filling that position.

Seldom are there preset criteria with which to judge the success or failure of a lay leader. Once the position is filled there is such relief that a body is there, that nobody wants to rock the boat by actually looking to see if goals are being met and lives are being changed. The church is a perfect environment for a person lacking leadership qualifications and experience, but consumed by an obsession to lead the troops.

Those who are not able to compete successfully in the world's arena are pleasantly surprised when they step into the body of Christ and find that if they counterfeit the appearance of a growing Christian closely enough, they are soon given authority over other growing Christians.

The Habitual Leader

Secular leadership tends to have a generic quality about it. A natural leader can function anywhere because leadership is an attitude, not a talent. It is an attitude of confidence, a willingness to make decisions, because the one who makes decisions is in control. If leadership is anything it is a quest for control, and control becomes a habit, maybe even an addiction.

The habitual leader's security and self-worth comes from the need to control people, projects, and organizations. He is a very functional individual and skilled at getting things accomplished. He sees the church as one more opportunity to wield power and authority. He is not afraid of making decisions and can live with the consequences of being wrong. He will establish and use a spiritual personality to assume positions of authority within the church structure.

When a habitual leader steps into the body of Christ, unless the Holy Spirit is in control of his life, the leader's personality will chafe under the authority of others and will either leave the body or take on those spiritual characteristics that will give him the power he craves.

Unlike the unrequited leader, the habitual leader seldom seeks out the church just to become a leader within its organization. He is usually a leader in business or the community, and many times finds himself part of a large or growing church because it is one more validation of him as a well-balanced community-minded person. It establishes him morally and ethically in the eyes of business associates and the community. Sometimes the chameleon will have grown up in a church where membership is more or less a family tradition.

For whatever the reason, he finds himself a member of an organization not operating as efficiently as he thinks it should, led by people who "obviously" do not make very good decisions and are focused on the wrong priorities most of the time. His perception is, "Isn't God fortunate to have me here, at this time and place to save the day?"

Charles officially joined his parent's church when he was nine years old and twenty years later became a deacon without much happening spiritually during those years. Two years later he moved because of his job and joined a young but growing church in his new neighborhood. This church seemed to be the best in town, and he wanted to be a part of it and get on the board of deacons as soon as possible. After all, they needed a man with his maturity and experience. Although Charles was a spiritual corpse he wasn't stupid, and he soon realized that this was an evangelistic church. He'd better start acting excited if he wanted to get anywhere. He began to attend Sunday school regularly and signed up for a home Bible study. He talked the talk and walked the walk.

It would be nice to give Charles the benefit of the doubt here, to believe that this body of Christ had shown Charles where he really was spiritually, and that a true conversion experience was a part of Charles's future. However, three months later Charles learned that a minimum of five years' membership was required before being considered as a candidate for deacon. Within a month he was attending another church with no time requirement for that position.

The leadership chameleon can be found in a variety of church environments. He is quickly accepted into churches where programs are more important than people, where the church is more of a functional institution than a relational institution. Under these circumstances a person's abilities can easily take precedent over concern about his spiritual character.

If a church puts on large musical or dramatic productions, a beautiful voice or a creative, theatrical background can overshadow spiritual substance. It is astonishing how easily we believe that a person has the spiritual character of an angel just because he can sing like one.

The leadership chameleon will ride the wave of his or her gift, looking strong, confident, purposeful. He has an energy that can easily be mistaken for spiritual commitment. If the people who are so impressed with this man's zeal for God on Sunday were to see him on Monday afternoon, they would see the same zeal directed at increasing the month's profit margin. Energy and excitement are generic qualities of the natural leader; they have no one product endorsement.

Because of his skills, the leadership chameleon may also be found in churches that have a very relational upper staff, with pastors and leaders who are more concerned for the people than the program. Every organization needs functional people, people who see that plans are made and carried out. It is difficult to meet the needs of the body without someone having the organizational skills to establish and facilitate a program and carry that process along with the energy and drive that will draw others into the project.

The relational leader operates in a different dimension than the functional leader. He sees people in terms of themselves, not their worth to the body. Before decisions are made or people are asked to commit to a course of action, the relational leader will spend time agonizing over the effects on all involved. The functional leader is more concerned with getting things accomplished, making the decision and living with whatever pressure, emotional, spiritual or other, that might come of the decision.

The relational leader will usually affect the body just as strongly as the functional leader and probably with more enduring results because he is building people's lives and not just programs. The functional leader, however, will be much more impressive because he seems to accomplish more in less time. As a result, the relational pastor may stand in awe of a functional lay leader, seeing in him a more effective ministry personality, more dynamic even to the point of allowing him a significant amount of authority.

A functional lay leader with a personal relationship with Christ, growing and becoming more like Him, will be softened and controlled by what Galatians 5:22–23 calls the fruit of the Spirit: "love, joy, peace, longsuffering, kindness, goodness, faithfulness, gentleness, self-control. Against such there is no law." Extraordinary things can happen in a purposeful, decisive man when patience, kindness, and gentleness flow

through his life. And destruction can follow as
easily, when the restraining power of the Holy
Spirit is not present in functional leaders.

I believe that a majority of the divisions
within churches come about because people are
given positions of spiritual authority who have
never learned what it is to be a servant, because
they have never learned to serve the greatest Servant of all. They attained power and control, and
when the inevitable happened and they disagreed
with the direction the pastoral staff decided to
take, the battle began.

How does the body of Christ protect itself
from leaders who are leading with the wrong mo-
tives? How does it protect itself from leaders who
are focused on their own needs more than the
needs of those over whom they have been given
charge? There are 478 answers to this question
throughout the pages of Scripture; that is exactly
how many times the word *servant* appears in the
Bible. Jesus laid out specific conditions for those
who claim a leadership role in the body of believers when He said, "You know that the rulers of the
Gentiles lord it over them, and those who are
great exercise authority over them. Yet it shall not
be so among you; but whoever desires to become
great among you, let him be your servant. And
whoever desires to be first among you, let him be
your slave—just as the Son of Man did not come
to be served, but to serve, and to give His life a
ransom for many" (Matt. 20:25–28).

There is no qualification sufficient to justify becoming a leader unless the heart of a servant has shown through first. Christ makes this
clear. And it is not as if churches do not have
adequate opportunities for people to display a
servant's heart. I know Modesto First Baptist had
little trouble testing mine.

After about six months of attending worship services and the singles' Sunday school class,
the evening program coordinator approached me
and asked if I would like to be a member of the
committee that planned the Sunday evening programs for the singles. I gladly agreed to help, and
the coordinator then sat down and asked me a few
questions. Was I a member of the church? Was I
attending morning and evening services regularly? Was I attending Sunday school regularly?
That was the first filter that I was sifted through as
I became a functioning member of the singles'
staff.

I had been a teacher for twelve years, coordinated an outdoor education program for three
schools, and was the president of the local chapter
of the California Teachers Association. Lurking
somewhere within the inner recesses of my soul a
small voice whispered, "Once they find out how
capable I am, they are really going to feel fortunate that I decided to attend this church."

The purpose of the evening program committee was to originate and implement creative
programs, from informative guest speakers to

panels on "hot" topics, to skits, dramas, musicals, and everything in between; what a job for a creative guy like me.

For the next four months, I set up chairs before the program and took them down after the program. You have to understand, I wasn't in charge of chairs, I was under someone who was in charge of chairs. After four months in chairs, I was promoted to moving the piano for a couple of months. Somewhere between the chairs and the piano I began to cling to Romans 7:6: "But now we have been delivered from the law, having died to what we were held by, so that we should serve in the newness of the Spirit and not in the oldness of the letter."

Finally, someone on the committee saw this tragic waste of creative talent and gave me doughnut-duty for Sunday mornings.

I don't think anyone doubted my ability to be creative, innovative, and capable, but I did need to develop a servant's heart. Serving Him was more important than proclaiming Terry Benner as the blessing this church had been awaiting. This was the second level of sifting.

Over that six–month period, I learned to serve joyfully no matter what I was doing, and the staff found that I did have a servant's heart even if I did tend to think more of myself than any person in his or her right spiritual mind should. Two weeks later I was asked to create and coordinate a program on expectations. Someone obviously felt

I had become quite familiar with the subject over the past several months.

As I mentioned, I am a teacher by profession and, I feel, a very good one. I know this is the gift the Lord has given me. During the next two years in singles I did everything but teach. I became coordinator of evening programs; after that, I coordinated our men's ministry and small discipleship groups. Finally, I was asked to teach our two leadership classes and, in time, became our Sunday school coordinator overseeing anywhere from eight to ten classes.

In our church ministry we encourage people to move in a different direction from where their gift would take them for several reasons. The first is that we get very comfortable and self-reliant where we are gifted, where we do well. It's too easy to think, I do this so well and so easily, why bother the Lord with it? We don't need to pray when we already know what to do, or so we lead ourselves to believe.

The second reason is that it allows us to rub up against people who have different gifts from ours. When this happens we learn to relate to different types of people, and we learn from the gifts they have. I am one of those people who is functional and not relational. When I began to coordinate the men's ministry, I quickly realized that I had few relational skills, so I prayed for a man to disciple me and the Lord provided one who was to become an intimate friend.

I always grow more when I find myself in areas where I am weak. In 2 Corinthians 12:9–10 Paul says, "And [Jesus] said to me, 'My grace is sufficient for you, for My strength is made perfect in weakness.' Therefore most gladly I will rather boast in my infirmities, that the power of Christ may rest upon me. Therefore I take pleasure in infirmities, in reproaches, in needs, in persecutions, in distresses, for Christ's sake. For when I am weak, then I am strong."

Redirecting a person for a time also gives the staff a good read on that person's spiritual maturity. The issue of obedience is nonexistent as long as a person is doing what he wants or what comes easily. Asking someone to be obedient means that they would prefer to do something else, otherwise obedience would not be necessary. Asking a person who is a gifted singer to work in the children's ministry with the toddlers or a teacher to move chairs or a Bible study leader to usher helps identify the chameleon. When the color he's sitting on changes, he suddenly feels very insecure.

"And I will pray the Father, and He will give you another Helper, that He may abide with you forever—the Spirit of truth, whom the world cannot receive, because it neither sees Him nor knows Him; but you know Him, for He dwells with you and will be in you. . . . But the Helper, the Holy Spirit, whom the Father will send in My name, He will teach you all things, and bring to

your remembrance all things that I said to you"
(John 14:16–17, 26).

The power and the guidance of the Holy
Spirit allow believers to step into alien environments with a sense of security, not in themselves
but in God's commitment to them. The gift isn't
the issue for the believer who is filled with the
Holy Spirit; serving is. Where can I serve, should
be the question, not how can I use my gift. If you
are able to serve in the area of your gift that's
great, but the use of your gift should never dictate
whether or not you are going to serve.

For the leadership chameleon, it is the gift
that is his passport into the position of authority.
When he is put into a situation where his gift can
no longer support and validate him, without the
Holy Spirit he becomes disoriented, frustrated,
then angry.

Philippians 2:3–9 says, "Let nothing be
done through selfish ambition or conceit, but in
lowliness of mind let each esteem others better
than himself. Let each of you look out not only for
his own interests, but also for the interests of
others. Let this mind be in you which was also in
Christ Jesus, who, being in the form of God, did
not consider it robbery to be equal with God, but
made Himself of no reputation, taking the form of
a bondservant, and coming in the likeness of men.
And being found in appearance as a man, He
humbled Himself and became obedient to the
point of death, even the death of the cross. There-

fore God also has highly exalted Him and given Him the name which is above every name."

Before members of the body are allowed to step into positions of authority the church should sift them through various programs and ministries to test their servant's heart. See how they respond under others' authority in tasks and circumstances that have little glamour or excitement. It is important to test the servant's heart before establishing a leader's authority.

PART THREE

PEELING OFF THE PAINT

WITH TIME, PATIENCE, AND A WELL-TUNED PIANO,

Eventually, the Colors Fade

I REMEMBER ONCE reading in an educational publication about a study done with preschool children. They took twenty children and during morning recess placed them in a large grassy area, approximately an acre in size, with no fence or border around it. They played there for thirty minutes with freedom to move wherever they would like within that given area. By the end of recess the twenty youngsters were huddled in a tight group in the center of the field playing together.

Over the next several days the acre was completely fenced in and once more the children were allowed out to play. The observers noted a marked difference in the movement of the chil-

dren. Whereas before they had stayed close together in the middle of the field, it was now ob-
served that the children ran all over the acre,
many playing by themselves, some even climbing
on the fence itself, evidently much more comfortable and secure in their environment.

All of us need the security of boundaries in
our lives. In fact almost every facet of our lives is
controlled, in some way, by limits and boundaries
except for the areas of our personal relationships.
There exists almost a state of anarchy in the relational world today with few guidelines and only
the limits of our own moral disposition to put a
hedge around our lives.

I believe that's why talk shows, like Phil
Donahue and Oprah Winfrey, are so popular.
People are wandering around on this relational
playground looking for the fence, looking for a
boundary line or a rule book to give them some
kind of security while they play the relational
game. People come into our ministry every day,
bruised and battered emotionally and spiritually
because they were in a game where there were no
rules, no referee, and no sense of fair play. It's
amazing how many of them step right back into
that game, simply because it's the only game in
town.

The spiritual chameleon loves the absence
of rules, because then who can say what's right or
wrong, what's honest or dishonest, acceptable or
unacceptable. The main purpose of camouflage is

to blur lines of distinction so that there is no clear outline of the individual who is trying to hide. God does not want us making choices out of confusion and ignorance, but with the strength of knowledge and discernment.

Given the perfect environment, I am gifted with a fine singing voice. I am continually amazed that someone has yet to discover this. I even have my own sound studio, completely tiled, with piped–in hot and cold running water. While singing in this unique sound studio, the richness and fullness of my voice is an experience not to be missed. However, we have a rather small hot-water heater and, if I stand in the shower long enough, my voice gets progressively higher as the water temperature gets lower.

Even outside of my personal studio I am capable of convincing myself that, as I sing along with the radio, they could just as easily substitute my voice for the one on the record and not a soul would notice the difference. Reality sets in as I ride along singing in the car with Jo Ann, who was a music major in college. I realize that one of us is out of key and chances are it's not her. Thank goodness Jo Ann is a kind and gentle woman who says very little about the discrepancy in our two voices. At times she may even imply that she enjoys my singing. This assures me that there is still eromania left in our marriage. I have noticed, however, that a small tic develops in her left eye after an especially long trip.

Even if Jo Ann were to say, "Terry, your singing ability falls somewhere between Chinese water torture and the groans of a water buffalo in labor," I could choose to ignore her subtle response to my singing with the following rationalizations: she has a tin ear; she is obviously jealous of someone who has less training but a better voice; she's mad about something and taking it out on my singing.

As long as I use my standards, or even another person, to evaluate my singing ability the verdict can be dismissed, or at least questioned, because the evaluation is filtered through prejudices, expectations, and desires; in other words, it's subjective.

The bottom line is that for others to get a clear, trustworthy, believable read on my singing ability I must place myself in an environment that will compare my voice with an objective and accepted standard of what a good voice should be. If I were to try out for the choir I would have to audition with the choir director who would, when certain notes were played on a tuned piano, require me to match those notes with my voice. He would use an objective scale to get a true read on my voice.

Time forced me out of the shower, which allowed me to pretend I was a better singer than I was. After so many minutes the environment changed because I'd run out of hot water. Time forced me into an environment where my weaknesses could not be covered up by a tile echo chamber and the sound of running water.

When a chameleon spends several months in a Bible study, he can appear very knowledgeable and spiritually on track, just by using the right language and sharing the right experiences. He is operating in an environment that provides very useful camouflage, as the shower did for my singing. If one evening the Bible study decides to go door-to-door, sharing Christ, the environment has changed and the chameleon is left sitting on a different background. Suddenly his implied wisdom, experience, and maturity is focused on practical application. He is asked to sing a spiritual melody in the presence of others when it is doubtful that he can even carry a tune.

For one who likes to pretend, time is not a friend. Time is, in fact, one of two very useful tools in neutralizing a chameleon's camouflage, for in time all colors fade. Whether it is a friendship, a financial interaction, a romance, or a leadership decision, time is our ally and the most effective tool in identifying a chameleon.

Whatever the issue, if the decision to move ahead toward commitment can be slowed so that both people have a chance to study and learn about each other's characteristics, habits, and behavior, then whatever camouflage might be in place can, in most cases, be neutralized. The more knowledge we have of a person, the better decisions we can make about what commitments we make to them. We are always trapped into assuming if we do not have sufficient information. The problem is how to gain information so that we can make good, informed decisions.

Encouraging the Colors to Fade

One summer I worked as a naturalist for a county science camp in the Sierra Nevada of California. One of the exercises was a hike where the students collected insects in small bottles and brought them back to camp for display and discussion, eventually releasing them. The small prisoners ranged from common beetles and ants to much more interesting creatures, such as centipedes and scorpions, with an occasional snake thrown in for good measure.

For the first few weeks I was what you might call an apprentice naturalist and went out with the veteran until I learned the ropes. When we returned to camp for lunch, the veteran had the students sit in a large circle, open the jars, one by one, take the creatures out, and discuss its life cycle and anything peculiar or special about the animal. It made no difference what kind of animal it was, beetle and scorpion got the same treatment. He would shake them out of the jar and hold them on his hand while we discussed them. As I said earlier I have this problem with things that crawl or slither, especially things that crawl, slither, and bite. Being a macho kind of guy, how-ever, and seeing that the little beasties looked pretty docile I figured I could handle it.

My first solo hike went great, and by the time we got back to camp and had lunch I was feeling rather pleased with myself. I had left the animals in my room, awaiting their debut. It was a quiet place and I definitely didn't need agitated animals for "show and tell."

After the students were seated and quiet I retrieved the first jar. It contained a centipede, approximately an inch long, that looked about as docile as a hyperactive child who had three Her-shey bars for breakfast.

As soon as the centipede hit the palm of my hand I knew I was in trouble. In the distance be-tween the jar and my palm he managed to get all one hundred legs moving and left little invisible footy-prints up the lifeline of my outstretched palm, made a sharp left at my wrist, and raced with all-out abandon under the cuff of my long-sleeve shirt.

During the next few minutes the students did not pick up much usable information concern-ing centipedes, but they had a unique lesson in human physiology as the centipede made a quick geographical survey of my entire body.

Alfred Hitchcock spent most of his life as a film director trying to create the expression that appeared on my face. It wasn't your common, everyday gut-wrenching panic. No, there was a kind of desperate sincerity about it, an inner beauty if you will. That macho, stoic expression that I had developed and come to count on now strove to go where no expression had gone before. What I did with my mouth alone was quite impressive, not to mention the spontaneous pupil dilation and hair rigidity. I was bitten three times in what I considered strategic locations, which I know my little friend must have taken some training course to find.

Later that afternoon I shared my experience with the "veteran." He was a man of extraordinary emotional control, and after moving through a series of camouflaged smirks, uncontrolled giggling, and gut-ripping guffaws, he was able to wipe away the tears, take several gulps of air, and tell me where I went wrong.

"Didn't you notice what I did with the jars, once we got back to camp?" he asked.

"Well, I just assumed you put them someplace quiet until it was time for the lesson."

"I put them someplace quiet all right," said the veteran, "I put them in the refrigerator. Think boy, these are cold-blooded animals; their bodies take on the temperature of their surroundings. By the time they've spent an hour at thirty-five degrees they move about as fast as molasses in January. Why, you'd never get me to put one of them critters on my hand when they've been at room temperature; a man could get bit that way. I don't know how I forgot to tell you that. Of course, I've been forgetting to tell that to each new naturalist for the last ten years. Must be just a bad habit I've gotten into." He made this last statement with a mischievous wink.

The speed with which a relationship travels is controlled by the amount of time the couple spends alone together. The more time they spend alone, the faster the relationship moves from the acquaintance stage to being sexually intimate. If you saw the time it took that centipede to cover my body, and the time it takes a couple, who spend most of their time together alone, to move from acquaintance to either marriage or sexual intimacy, put your money on the couple. The centipede has only a hundred fast little legs, but a couple has eromania, which fuels and energizes the need to spend time alone.

Had I asked the students to give me detailed information about the centipede's behavioral characteristics or physical appearance, little information would have been forthcoming. All they saw was a blur due to the speed with which the animal moved. The romantic chameleon loves speed. The faster the relationship goes, the less the victim is able to see and understand, and the more effective the chameleon's camouflage can be.

The old naturalist knew the key: Whatever you want to get a good look at, slow it down. After placing the creature in the refrigerator, the cold slowed it down enough for him and his students

to be able to see it clearly, and study its characteristics, habits, and behavior; to become intimately
familiar with the object of their interest.

As it is with a centipede, so it is with a
relationship; it needs to be slowed to give both
people the opportunity to study and learn about
each other. For the centipede, cold was the ele-
ment that slowed him down; for the spiritual chameleon, the magical mixture is time plus friendship.

We have a lot of filters in our lives through
which we look at others. How we see them and
what we look for depends upon the filter we use.
If we use a romantic filter our focus centers on
such things as looks, personality, how well the
individual entertains us, how good he or she
makes us feel about ourselves, and of course, the
biggie, what kind of marriage partner he or she
might make.

Friendship has a slightly different type of
filter, for we must depend upon our friends, but
not necessarily upon our lovers. Friendship looks
through a grid of trust, endurance, compassion,
forgiveness, acceptance, spiritual discernment,
and wanting the very best for that person in all
things, whether it involves you as a friend or not.

What I've just described are the properties
of a close friendship. In a close friendship we take
responsibility for the other person's life. We think
about them and pray about them when they are
not around. We see the potential in their lives and

encourage, exhort, and help them to realize those possibilities, and allow them to do the same in our lives. There is a willingness to be vulnerable, but along with that vulnerability is a desire to minister to that person and allow oneself to be ministered to in return.

The intimate friendship goes further in that it is based on an unconditional acceptance of the other person. No matter what you do or say, or how you feel about me, I will be your friend. If there comes a time when you refuse to recipro-cate my friendship, it will not affect how I feel about you. When two people come to this under-standing within a friendship, it allows the free-dom of confrontation. As Proverbs 27:17 says, "As iron sharpens iron,/So a man sharpens the countenance of his friend."

It is a depressing reality, but romantic er-omania inhibits the process of friendship; on the other hand, friendship slows down the process of eromania. They have a difficult time occupying the same space at the same time. How then do we deal with this emotional monster that walks across our relational lives like Godzilla tiptoeing through Gotham City? What is the key that turns Godzilla into Puff the Magic Dragon and makes romantic love an exciting adventure, instead of a never-ending journey through a junkyard filled with '59 Edsels?

We are seldom asked for an opinion on this, but when inquiring minds want to know we tell them we think a close friendship should be a prerequisite for a romantic relationship. Of course, it takes a while for two people to develop a friendship of this nature and that warms the hearts of those of us on staff.

Remember, the one variable that controls the speed with which a relationship develops is time together, alone. We do not have a refrigerator to put these two people in, but we do have a special environment available to those who feel more comfortable moving in slow motion as opposed to fast-forward.

Friendship Before Romance

About ten years ago Jim wondered why someone wasn't doing something about this issue of friendship-before-relationship. Realizing that he was "someone," he put together a two-part guide for individuals who decide to visit the land of friendships and relationships. The first part is entitled the "Friendship Commitment."

The purpose of the opposite-sex Friendship Commitment is to allow men and women to learn how to become friends within the safety of an established structure having guidelines and limits. The form on pages 154–155 is the commitment itself. A couple wishing to become better acquainted with each other, without getting tangled up in a romantic relationship, is given the

opportunity of signing a four–month commitment to establish a viable friendship. At the end
of the four months the couple may choose to ex-
tend the commitment, continue to work on the
friendship without the official structure, or go on
to a more serious relationship, for which we have
a "Part II" of the guidebook. For now however,
let's take a brief look at "Part I."

The commitment we are about to discuss
has been used in the singles' and career groups
for more than ten years, and well over a hundred
couples have completed it, many going on to
more serious relationships and then marriage,
others coming to the realization that they wanted
to remain friends only.

Commitment to Build a Genuine Opposite-Sex Friendship

GOALS:

1. To promote spiritual maturity through encouraging one another in worship and service to Jesus Christ. (see Colossians 2:2–3)
2. To develop and express agape love, God's love to others. (see 1 Corinthians 13:4–8)
3. To learn to control physical, emotional, and mental habits. (see 1 Thessalonians 4:4–6)
4. To build trust, integrity, and transparency. (see Proverbs 17:9)

LIMITS:

1. If you are not legally divorced you may not enter into an opposite-sex friendship.
2. No physical touching (hand-holding, arm-in-arm, etc.).
3. Because of time requirement there should be no dating during the commitment period.

TIME:

1. *Four* months (minimum).
2. *Twenty-five* hours maximum per month; *Fifteen* hours minimum time per month.
3. Group time to equal one-fourth time alone (interacting with others in a group situation).
4. Phone time as full time after a half-hour.

THINGS TO DO:

1. Share goals, needs, struggles, and victories.
2. Bible study, prayer, Scripture memorization.
3. Read and discuss, *Friends and Friendship* by White, or *Quality Friendship* by Gary Inrig.

4. Help each other with projects.
5. Be creative and original in planning your time together. All costs are shared equally.
6. Have fun and enjoy yourselves.

THINGS TO AVOID:
1. All talk of relationship and marriage.
2. Too much contact with engaged or married couples.
3. Intimate or cozy atmosphere.
4. Romantic movies, gifts, cards, compliments.
5. Too much emphasis on heavy, personal problems to the extent that they dominate the friendship.

If the physical boundaries which are set by this agreement are exceeded, I agree to inform someone who is a spiritual authority in my life (Sunday school teacher, Bible study leader, ministry coordinator, or pastor) that this has happened.

STARTING DATE_____

ENDING DATE (Four months

later)_____(midnight)

SIGNED_____

SIGNED_____

Remember at the first of this chapter I discussed my singing ability. I alluded to the fact that the only way I can get an objective look at how well I sing is to match my voice with an objective standard, such as a scale of notes played on a piano. The above commitment is a willingness of two people to place themselves in an environment that will slow the relationship, because it controls time spent together alone. It also gives each person some clear, objective guidelines with which to assess the other person. Let's take a closer look at this scale of relational notes.

Goals

The first aim is to create a spiritual foundation for the friendship. Many people have never been ministered to by a Christian friend; nor had an opportunity to minister to anyone else. Although friendships can and should be a lot of fun, the issue of agape love—God's love—implies that I am not here just to have fun, but to make a difference in your life for Jesus Christ.

The second goal is learning to open my life to another human being, to risk showing who I really am, sharing not only my past struggles and failures, but what I am contending with now, my fears and weaknesses. If I am being open I must also share the growth in my life, how God changes me, sharing with my friend the gifts and blessings God has allowed in my life. Trust will not come before there has been some risk taken and survived. Integrity cannot be established unless truth has been shared.

Limits

Many people have what we call emotional divorces. Their spouse left them three months ago; they've gone through twelve weeks of emotional adjustment, cried all they think they are going to cry, felt all they think they are capable of feeling, and come to the conclusion that it's time to get on with life. They believe they have emotionally put their marriage behind them, and begin looking for a new relationship.

Within our singles' body the focus—though we often fail—is to honor God and be a witness before the world in all we say and do; this includes our relationships. If a person has not received his final decree of divorce he is, in the state of California, and more importantly in the eyes of God, still married and should act married. Therefore, when people are separated but not yet divorced, we encourage them to have a same-sex friendship, but we do not make opposite-sex friendships available to them. Although friendship is genderless, we feel that anything that might become an obstacle to the reconciliation of the marriage should be avoided at all costs.

The line that separates friendship from romance is the physical aspect; once you hold hands, kiss, or embrace each other you step from friendship into relationship. It's like the young man in our high school group who shared one evening about a girl he had grown up with. She was his next–door neighbor; they went to the same school and over the years shared much. One evening while baby-sitting her younger brother they got into a wrestling match on the living room floor. One thing led to another, they found themselves in an embrace, and kissed. Recalling the event he said, "You know, it was never the same between us again. Everything we thought and felt toward one another was changed in an instant."

I played poker when I was in college. I was fairly conservative, but one guy in our dorm got a little crazy every time he played. If it was his turn to deal, at least four cards in the deck would be wild. What was before was no longer; a deuce, a one-eyed jack, an ace, and the queen of spades looked like the same card, but could change depending on the hand I held. It became difficult to keep up with what was what. When we move from friendship into relationship all the cards go wild, and what was before is no longer. In a romantic relationship a simple statement such as "I like children," is translated, "I want you to marry me and have my children." If you are committed to being a friend and begin to do physical things with that person, it creates expectations that have nothing to do with friendship.

Time

Time is probably the most important factor requiring boundaries and structure. As stated before, the one variable that controls how fast a relationship develops is time spent alone together. Some of the friendships in our singles' ministry happen because people just want to establish another friend. Sometimes a more mature believer is asked to do a friendship with a younger believer as part of the ministry; most, however, come about because there is some kind of a relational attraction, even to the point of eromania, that draws the two people into the commitment.

The limit on time spent together is what slows the natural momentum of the relationship. It stretches a hundred hours of time spent alone together over four months. It allows time for other people and circumstances to flow across both people's lives, permitting each of them to see how the other responds to various situations, and to each other. Over the years the greatest struggle I have seen in the relational area is the battle for patience, to allow God time to work out His plan in your life.

Things to Do

Well, if you can't do all the fun stuff, like kissing and cuddling and your everyday common variety necking, what can you do for four months that will seem at least slightly more exciting than

reruns of "Bonanza"? I think this is where planning and creativity come into focus. Because of
the limits placed on your time together, time itself
becomes a valuable commodity.

Many of the couples spend some of their
time planning the rest of their time. It becomes
important to talk about what you enjoy and what
you don't, what things you've never done that
you'd like to do, and that you share that experience with your friend.

Jo Ann and I grew up in the same area, so
when we went through a friendship commitment
we decided that for our first time out together we
would spend the day taking each other to two or
three places that had been very special to us while
growing up. It was a great day, a lot of fun, and we
learned some things about each other that we
might not have known for a long time, had we
relied solely on casual conversation.

Working on projects together can be a
good way to get to know each other and get some
things accomplished at the same time. After
spending two or three hours together painting a
room or cleaning up the yard, we tend not to look
quite as nice, smell as sweet, or be as congenial,
especially if we don't agree on how the work
should be done.

A project gives us neutral ground on which
to interact with the other person. It creates a comfortable atmosphere in which the conversation

can revolve around the activity and not be so obsessively focused on each other.

In the ongoing process of friendship the disclosing of one to another should occur naturally, and not be forced or coerced. If there isn't a lot of laughter, relaxation, and a sense of playfulness in the friendship, then a large part of what the friendship should and could do in your life is not going to be realized.

Things to Avoid

When there is a romantic attraction it's tough to remember one is working on a friendship. The hardest part to control is our imagination: the daydreams and fantasies, the hopeful expectations about this person. These are not wrong in themselves, but when they dominate our thought life, interfere with our quiet time with the Lord and our prayer life, then things get a little weird. In ministry that's exactly what we call it, getting the weirds.

There are several things that will help stimulate the weirds. One is just casual conversation about romance and marriage. Another is spending a lot of time with engaged or married couples. Engaged couples tend to ooze eromania and anyone who finds himself in the same vicinity as an engaged couple can drown in the emotional overflow.

Although there is little scientific evidence, there seems to be a correlation between the length of time a couple has been married and the dissipation of eromania, so eromania seems not to be a factor in hanging around married couples. However, the longer a couple has been married seems to be directly proportional to the degree of insistence by both spouses that everyone around them, friends or relatives, get married.

Ambiance can also create the weirds. After a romantic movie it's difficult not to talk about romance. There's nothing wrong with sending a card of appreciation to a friend; however, we must understand that there is a difference between praise and flattery.

Praise is given to encourage, to express appreciation; praise expects nothing in return, it is entirely for the other person. Flattery has a selfish motive; it does expect something in return, either an emotional response or, at the very least, a compliment in return. It is the difference between saying to a person, "Thank you for being a prayer warrior in my life. You have shown me how special that can be," and "You've got the most beautiful blue eyes." Both may be true statements, but only one would be said to a friend. Remember, we are not told to flatter God, but to praise Him.

There are at least four things this commitment will do for one as a single person and as a Christian. The first is that it will allow a person to experience, within the safety and security of its boundaries, what it's like to have an opposite-sex friend. Possibly you have already been blessed with that experience, but many have not. We have men and women who have been through a multitude of relationships, never able to call any of them a friend. Within the security of the commitment you will feel a marvelous freedom to express who you are.

I have always said that dating is the process of gathering information with which you will make relational choices. The problem with dating is that one misunderstood statement, forgotten appointment, or unfulfilled expectation can end the relationship without an opportunity to resolve or clarify the problem. The information gathering stops and you may have wanted to get or give more information. Within the commitment you know that no matter what, you have four months in this person's life. You don't have to worry about issues like, will he/she kiss me good night; if she doesn't, does she like me; if I don't, will he call me again; is he going out with me because he expects sex; if we don't have sex, will it end the relationship?

One thing I tell women is that if a man is willing to commit to spend four months without the possibility of any physical touching or caressing, you can be pretty sure he's interested in more than just your body.

The second thing it does for those who are already romantically attracted to one another is to take romance to a level that most people, in our society today, never have the pleasure of experiencing. William Butler Yeats said, "Desire dies because every touch consumes." In the world today it is assumed that sexual attraction and intimacy is a prerequisite to romance, with many feeling that the terms are synonymous. Sexual familiarity strangles romance.

When I went through this commitment with Jo Ann, at the end of the four months just being able to hold her hand was exciting, and a simple kiss was very special. Before I became a Christian I had spent a lot of time in the world, yet at the end of those four months I felt like a high school kid on his first date. Those things that the world pushes aside, ignores, and sometimes even scorns, God says are jewels, if you'll only take the time to turn them in His Light.

The third thing, and I believe the most important, is that it will give you a four–month spiritual read on the person in whom you are interested. For the Christian, the bottom line of friendship, romantic relationships, and especially marriage, is that every time you make a commitment, you are making three commitments: one to yourself, one to the other person, and one to Christ. How does your friend honor the commitment he has made? Does he initiate instead of follow? Are you the one who is always suggesting you pray about an issue, or who reminds the other that you haven't studied the Word together in quite a while? Are you the one who is having to control the physical side of the friendship, or the time limits?

It is not that there should be an expectation of perfection within the commitment. There may well be struggles and failure, but how is the struggle and failure dealt with? Many times I have had a man come to me and say, "Terry, I'm having a real struggle keeping the physical part of this commitment; in fact, Mary and I held hands the other evening."

Now I know you're probably saying, "Well big deal," but it is a big deal. James 4:17 says, "Therefore, to one who knows the right thing to do, and does not do it, to him it is sin" (NAS). Before this man made the commitment, holding hands was fine. But once the commitment was made, the good he knew he should do was in keeping his pledge not to become physically involved with this woman; when he did it, he realized it was sin. But he then did the right thing—he took spiritual responsibility for his action.

When this happens, I usually ask if the couple have asked each other's forgiveness and gone before the Lord and asked His forgiveness? If they have, I will ask if they need me to help them be accountable in this area, and will do so if asked. It is not the failure that we want to focus on so much as the desire of the heart and the response of the individual to the failure. Many times this allows us to see if Jesus Christ is alive and well and living within an individual.

I know it may seem that we are overreacting to a couple's simply holding hands, but before we initiated the friendship agreement in our ministry this same scenario was being played out over and over again, only the couples were not holding hands but sleeping together. It is amazing how a few boundary lines can create, not a spiritual prison, but a spiritual refuge.

Four months and the requirements of the commitment are like putting the spiritual chameleon inside a kaleidoscope of changing colors and images. God, however, does not want us to have to choose simply between what is acceptable or not acceptable; that's not what abundant life is about. In his book, *Quality Friendship,* Gary Inrig makes an important comment on this. He says, "I have learned that my biggest problem is not distinguishing between what is good and what is bad. It is seeing the difference between what is good, what is better, and what is best."

Within the multitude of Christian singles' groups throughout this country there is a tremendous number of people who love the Lord Jesus Christ with all their hearts, who have made Him Lord of their lives and are serving Him with excitement and dedication. In developing spiritual discernment and a patient spirit you will allow God to surround you with these types of people, first as friends and then possibly, even one to serve within the covenant of marriage.

Chapter 9

LEARNING THE NOTES: Practice, Practice, Practice

IN AN OPPOSITE-sex friendship romantic over-tones tend to push the level of commitment into areas where the friendship has not yet gone. Many couples are engaged to be married and have yet to establish a close, much less intimate friendship. Once engaged, the couple finds that the pressure and dynamics of the commitment force them into areas of vulnerability usually associated with closer relationships. In other words, the cart of commitment is pulling the horse of friendship.

In same-sex friendships this pressure is less intense. Many same-sex friends float along casually for years believing they are close just because they've known each other for so long. Many are content to keep the friendship at this nonchalant level. If you are a nonbeliever and have never known genuine, close friendship, you are missing one of the best experiences of life. If you are a Christian, the tragedy goes much further than just a missed relational experience.

Taking a Look at Mark and Dave

Mark came into the singles' group a year before Dave. Both loved to fish and hunt and were friends within a few months. Mark was fairly outgoing, whereas Dave was rather shy and quiet. Mark was well established socially in the group and involved in several things. Dave was not only new, but struggling from the very beginning.

I've never played much basketball because I resemble a pregnant hippo on the court. Dave handled conversation about as well as I handle a fast break. He hated to have attention drawn to himself. He wanted either to be alone or in a group of at least fifty so he could become lost in the crowd. We had talked several times about this, and he knew that in order to reach people for Christ he would have to talk to them. He was trying his best to change. He was struggling, but I would call it a good struggle because its purpose was to please the Lord of his life.

Mark was not struggling and that was the problem. Since he first stepped into the group he seemed satisfied with most things in particular and everything in general. Dave liked being with

Mark. They shared experiences in the field, and that gave Dave something he could talk about comfortably. I became a little concerned about Dave's dependence on Mark to the exclusion of others in the group, especially since I had been a bit troubled about Mark's spiritual health for some time. One morning over coffee I shared that concern with Dave.

"But he's my best friend, Terry. I can talk to him." Dave spoke more intensely than I'd expected. "A best friend, a close friend makes a spiritual difference in his friend's life," I said. "When was the last time you and Mark prayed together?"

"We have, I just can't exactly remember the last time," Dave answered.

"Do you ever talk about what the Lord is doing in your lives?"

"Sure, we talk about ministry a lot."

"Not ministry," I said, "about how Christ is changing your life, what you are struggling with, what you are excited about, how you can help each other."

"Mark doesn't seem to have that many problems," replied Dave, "so I feel funny about sharing mine."

"He has more problems than he thinks," I answered, "but that's not the issue. Is he making a difference in your life? Is he challenging you, helping you, encouraging you, confronting you when necessary so that you grow and mature in Christ? That's the issue."

"That's what a minister does."

"No Dave," I responded, "that's what a close, Christian friend does. I think you need to step out of Mark's life for a while and look for a friend who will do these things in your life and allow you to do them in his."

I had asked Dave to do a difficult thing, and though he reluctantly agreed that I was probably right, he couldn't bring himself to back away from the friendship.

We saw less and less of Mark as he became involved in professional bass fishing tournaments, which usually ran both Saturdays and Sundays. He had left the group having made little difference in anyone's life—except Dave's. In Dave's life he had wasted almost a year of a young Christian's opportunity to experience what being a friend in Christ is all about in order to have a fishing partner.

Dave had assumed that because Mark was an older Christian, he would fill the role of whatever a Christian friend was supposed to be. Dave had no objective criteria. He had experienced only casual friendships in the world and expected Christian friends to be the same.

Committing to Practice Friendships

What we like to do at First Baptist in Modesto is provide the young Christian with a sense of what should happen in a friendship with another believer. When it doesn't happen they can then at least ask why. It isn't that we expect Christians to be perfect friends; all of us need practice. But if we don't know what to practice, chances are there will not be much improvement.

In order to practice the skills for developing a friendship with a person of the same sex that encourages both of you to pursue and grow in Christ, you can use the friendship commitment from the previous chapter. The boundaries for the physical involvement won't be necessary, of course. But the goals and amount of time you will commit will be the same. You will be seeking to promote spiritual maturity by encouraging one another in worship and service to Jesus Christ. You will be learning to express God's love to others and building trust and integrity in a relationship with another believer, without spending so much time sharing heavy personal problems that they dominate your relationship. You will share goals, Bible study, and prayer, and read books on friendship, if you choose. But be sure you also leave time to have fun and enjoy yourselves.

When women from the singles' group come to us with an interest in a man, we typically ask if he has any close same-sex friends. If a man has not learned to develop a close friendship with another man, it will be difficult for him to do so with a woman. There is always an inner drive within an opposite-sex friendship—especially romantic relationships—to appear to be someone other than who you really are: to look better, sound smarter, appear more spiritual; to say "I am worthy of your attention." This is where the chameleon in each of us yells "Whoopie!" and turns three cartwheels and starts making plans.

Learning to say no to the chameleon in us is tough. The best place to practice is a same-sex friendship. There are fewer hidden agendas between two men or between two women. Our self-worth and self-image are not so wrapped up in how the other person views us. If we have difficulty being honest about ourselves with a friend of the same sex, we will find it almost impossible to do so with someone of the opposite sex. A man who finds it difficult to pray with another man, especially about issues he is struggling with, will find it more difficult to pray with a woman he wants to impress. The advantage of a good same-sex friend is that there is at least one person in our lives over whom the chameleon does not have power.

Bill and Eric had been close, Christian friends for more than two years. During the past year of the friendship, Bill shared with Eric that all of his adult life he had struggled with pornography; even as a Christian he had continued to struggle. For that year Eric had been intimately involved in helping Bill deal with the problem with a mixture of concern, love, accountability, and prayer. Bill knew that no matter what happened with this issue that Eric would not step back.

As the year progressed Bill began to develop a friendship with Sarah, one of the women in the singles' group. They grew closer and moved into a romantic relationship. Finally, Bill shared with Eric that he intended to ask Sarah to marry him. Eric asked Bill if he had told Sarah about the pornography issue and, of course, he had not. Bill intended to spend the rest of his life with this woman, to become "one" as Scripture says. His struggle was an issue that would directly impact their life together, yet he did not have the courage to confide in her. It wasn't that they were not spiritually close. In almost every area they had been open and vulnerable, both emotionally and spiritually. There was that one issue, however, that he could share with a close male friend but not with the woman he wanted to marry.

Eric confronted Bill about it, encouraged him to confide in Sarah and trust God that, whatever took place, it would be what God intended. Bill did as his friend asked. Understandably, Sarah had some real struggles accepting and dealing with what she was told. The engagement was put on hold; now there are two people involved in the process of freeing Bill of this issue in his life.

The very act of sharing with Sarah helped give Bill more support than he originally had. The fewer lives in which the chameleon has power to deceive, the less influence the chameleon has in our own lives.

Not only will a good same-sex friend lessen our need to hide and disguise ourselves, but he or she will also help tone down the colors in our other relationships, including in any role we have as a leader in the body of Christ.

Encouraging the Colors of the Leader to Fade

"Well, what do you think?"

The question was asked of seven people sitting around a large table in the conference room at church. I was one of the seven who sat in amazed silence. The person who had asked the question was Jim. The people who were asked were the administrative coordinators of the singles' ministry. Each of us had a major responsibility in the ministry and were responsible for anywhere from five to fifteen leaders, who functioned under us in various capacities.

Had the question dealt with ministry there would have been no hesitation in jumping in and hammering out a solution. We had immense freedom in making decisions concerning spiritual counsel, policy development, and ministry philosophy and direction. However, the question we now considered dealt not with ministry, but with our pastor's personal life.

For several years Jim had thought about pursuing his doctorate. Now he told us he was considering stepping into a doctoral program that summer. His question for us was, "Do you think I should?"

He went on to explain that he knew his decision would affect the ministry in terms of the time he could give it, and he understood it would also affect us. It was apparent that whatever he could not do we would have to pick up. This was not a simple question to be answered by a simple opinion. Jim made it clear that he would abide by our decision.

We discussed his plan for quite some time. Then Jim went around the table to each of us, and we said yes or no. The vote was four to three in favor of his pursuing the degree. At the next meeting Jim shared with us that he had decided to put the doctorate on hold. Many of the issues we had raised he had not considered. He felt this was not the best time to move in that direction.

In the room that day was a registered nurse, a farmer, a teacher, a college professor, a secretary, a social worker, a physical therapist, and one ordained pastor who had been in ministry for more than twenty years. He was a nationally–known author and speaker and was willing to let those seven other people decide the course of his life for the next several years.

There was nothing special about any of us that we should be given such a responsibility and privilege, except for the fact that a unique bond of spiritual trust existed between our pastor and ourselves. It was this trust that allowed him to place that decision in our hands. That trust was not an automatic by-product of the fact that we were Christians or members of the church, that we had shared a great testimony or had some significant spiritual experience. It was a trust born of time, patience, and an objective spiritual sifting process, which had helped to validate to ourselves and others, especially Jim, that each one of us had a genuine, growing relationship with the Lord Jesus Christ.

This sifting process showed not only our strengths and successes, but also our weaknesses and failures. Everyone sitting around that table had been in leadership in the singles' ministry for at least five years—some for more than fifteen years. Whatever bright colors we had initially flashed around had long since faded under the bright light of God's Word, the revelations of the Holy Spirit, and the love, encouragement, and confrontation of fellow workers. Time and patience had allowed all of these to flow across our lives. And as they had, we were able to see more clearly where we were in our walk with Christ, what we were willing to commit to because of that awareness, and what some of the issues were with which we still struggled. The third side of that triangle, in addition to time and patience, was the piano notes—the levels of leadership.

The first day each of us expressed an interest in moving into leadership, we were shown a levels of leadership form (page 178). It describes the levels of leadership that exist within the singles' ministry and the requirements to function at each level. Level three applies to those who have been a part of the singles' ministry for at least six months and have a desire to serve in some capacity. Level two is for those who have shown themselves to be faithful, available, and teachable and who desire challenge and growth in their walk through service in ministry. Level one is for those who have a desire to make the ministry of Jesus Christ a significant part of their lives. They are willing to step into areas outside their comfort zone and desire to open up and share their lives, the light and the dark, that others may benefit and grow as they themselves have.

Levels of Leadership

Level I

Servanthood Role

Administrative coordinator, Sunday school teachers, Prayer Room Counselor coordinators and interns

Requirements
1. Church member
2. Attend church, Sunday school, or PM program regularly
3. Actively support the staff policies
4. Signed job description
5. Completed or in a home Bible study
6. Refrain from drinking, smoking, or dancing
7. Commit to friendship, relationship, and pre-marital instruction
8. Agree to take the Taylor-Johnson Temperament Analysis Test
9. Tither who is encouraged to give to the building fund
10. Has completed Leadership I & II class

Level II

Serving Role

Committee member, Prayer Room Counselor

Requirements
1. Church member

2. Attend church, Sunday school, or PM program regularly
3. Conformity to the staff policies
4. Signed job description
5. Completed or in a home Bible study
6. Refrain from drinking, smoking, or dancing
7. Commit to friendship, relationship, and premarital instruction
8. Agree to take the T-JTA
9. Regular giver
10. Has completed or is in the process of completing Leadership I class

Level III

Minor Roles

Temporary jobs, set up, clean up—assigned by event

Requirements
1. Church member
2. Attend church, Sunday school, or PM program regularly
3. Be aware of staff policies

As you look at these levels and their corresponding requirements, your initial reaction may be that they are stifling and too restrictive. Remember that these are not requirements for being a Christian or belonging to the church or being a valued and appreciated part of the body of Christ. These apply *only to those who would step into positions of leadership* and have spiritual authority over others for teaching, discipling, and spiritual counseling.

There are some things on this form that the singles' ministry at Modesto First Baptist asks a leader to do and some things we ask leaders to refrain from doing. The things we ask may not always be spiritually life changing, but they are good, positive, proven steps in protecting and facilitating single Christians in their relationship with Christ and with others. How can a leader encourage others to participate in a Bible study if he has not taken part himself? Once again, are our colors real?

Not many people have a problem understanding the concern about drinking and smoking, but the dancing issue definitely gets a few toes indignantly tapping, including Al's.

Al had been involved in level three leadership for a year and in that time had grown considerably. I shared with Al a variety of ministries and programs available for his involvement—if he would be willing to step into the second level of leadership. Some time passed before he responded. Then one morning over coffee he said he wanted to move into some new areas of ministry, but there was one problem: He loved to dance to country-western music and didn't want to give it up.

I told him I understood, and if he wanted to stay at his current level, that was fine. There was nothing wrong with dancing. I also shared that at the level of leadership at which he wished to operate there would be people who had come out of the nightclub atmosphere and were trying to stay out of it; some were struggling with drug and alcohol abuse and the whole secular singles' environment. Although many of them enjoyed dancing, we encouraged them to step completely away from anything that might prove a hindrance to them. It is difficult to see a leader partake of the very thing that you have been denied. In Romans 15:1–2 Paul says, "We then who are strong ought to bear with the scruples of the weak, and not to please ourselves. Let each of us please his neighbor for his good, leading to edification."

Al said that he understood and that is why he had chosen to stay where he was. I finally asked Al what had happened to him this past year. Had there been any changes in his life? At that question he lit up and spent the next thirty minutes talking about all of the marvelous ways God had changed him and blessed his life. I then asked if he thought being involved in leadership had anything to do with that. A hint of realization crept into his eyes as he smiled and said, "Terry, you know it has. The people and challenges that have poured through my life this past year were due, in a great part, to serving others in this ministry."

"Al," I then said, "at the end of this year I will come to you and ask you these same questions. I'll be curious to learn just how much dancing every Saturday night for a year will have blessed and changed your life. And I will also ask you what you think you have missed out on, what could have happened if you had not made dancing more important than serving the Lord Jesus Christ in the most effective way you could."

Al looked at me, smiled, and said, "Those are going to be some pretty tough questions to answer, aren't they? Maybe I'd better think about it and pray a little bit more before I make a decision."

"All things are lawful for me, but all things are not helpful," Paul says in 1 Corinthians 6:12. "All things are lawful for me, but I will not be brought under the power of any." What the singles' leadership requirements had done was play a note for Al so he could see if he was hitting that note in his life. The real issue wasn't dancing but what was most important in Al's life. I didn't have to make that judgment, just play the note, and Al was able to hear his off-key response.

A few days later Al came to me with a willing and excited heart, anticipating what God was going to do in his life in the next year because of his commitment to move ahead and not be content to stay where he was. It would have been fine had he chosen to stay where he was. But he would have continued to talk about all the things God had done in his life for that one year, to rest in the brightness of colors which were but a memory.

As I write this, there is war in the Persian Gulf. In the daily newscasts and interviews, one issue seems to dominate the hearts and minds of the soldiers. It is the issue of their trust in the men who lead them; trust that they know what they are doing, that they have been trained and sifted, not only through the military ranks, but by experience. The soldiers who have been in combat, who have faced the enemy and survived, and who can pass that experience and knowledge on are the most highly valued.

Leadership in the body of Christ is serious business. It is the business of life and death, the business of war. Look at the following verses: "And war broke out in heaven: Michael and his angels fought with the dragon; and the dragon and his angels fought" (Rev. 12:7). "And the dragon was enraged with the woman, and he went to make war with the rest of her offspring, who keep the commandments of God and have the testimony of Jesus Christ" (Rev. 12:17). "He was given power to make war against the saints and to conquer them. And he was given authority over every tribe, people, language and nation" (Rev. 13:7, NIV). "They will make war against the Lamb, but the Lamb will overcome them because he is Lord of lords and King of kings—and with him will be his called, chosen, and faithful followers" (Rev. 17:14, NIV). "For though we live in the world, we do not wage war as the world does. The weapons we fight with are not the weapons of the world. On the contrary, they have divine power to demolish strongholds" (2 Cor. 10:3–4, NIV).

We who are believers in the Lord Jesus Christ are at war, living in occupied territory. The war in which we are engaged is of much greater magnitude than any war that has ever been fought on planet earth; it is for the eternal souls of all humanity. The leaders in this war must be just as capable and worthy of trust as those who lead soldiers in the Persian Gulf.

The sifting process that we use for leadership and the development of friendships with the same and opposite sex at Modesto First Baptist is not the answer for every church. But in every church there should be some process that allows our colors to fade; that provides time, patience, and an objective screen for us to see clearly who we are and who the people are we commit to in relationships so we won't be blinded by a rainbow of false colors.

Chapter 10

HEALING THE WOUNDS

JOE DECIDED TO take an afternoon walk through the foothills just above a lake where he had been fishing. The day was warm and Joe was dressed for it in shorts, a T-shirt, and tennis shoes. As he stepped over a small log on the path, he felt a sharp pain in his leg and thought he had scratched himself on a branch sticking out from the log. But he quickly dismissed this assumption when he noticed a large diamondback rattler slithering into the undergrowth beside the log.

Joe's heart sank as he looked down at his leg and saw that he was bleeding from two small puncture wounds in his right calf. "I must get to a hospital," he told himself. "But first, I'll find that blankety-blank snake and kill it!"

Joe spent precious minutes pushing aside the undergrowth, looking under logs, and turning over rocks in search of the snake. The venom quickly coursed through his body with the exertion of the search, leaving Joe dizzy and weak. He realized he was being foolish and turned to go back to his car. But after only a few steps, he collapsed on the path and lay there as the venom traveled to his heart, ending his life.

Hours later the sheriff found Joe's body and called the paramedics. They concluded that Joe had died of a snakebite, but they couldn't understand the reason; he had only been five minutes from his car and twenty minutes from the nearest hospital.

We can be so obsessed with the pain caused in our lives by chameleons that we will accept our own spiritual death if it means we can inflict as much suffering on them as they did on us. We can be consumed by bitterness, and exert so much effort focusing our anger on the person who hurt us that we commit spiritual suicide.

Finding Our Way Out of the Mire

Forgiveness is a peculiar principle. It seems to be at odds with our notion of fairness. We want to ensure that people treat us justly, or make them pay when they don't.

Payment can be made in a variety of currencies, but we, the injured party, feel we have the license to decide what the currency should be. It's often inexpensive; a simple apology will do. Revenge is always a popular denomination—"I don't get mad, I get even." We may seek to make people understand how badly they've hurt us before we accept an apology. Or we may reject all personal contact with them, even refusing to talk with them on the phone, to allow them a sample of what it would be like to lose us as a friend.

We can enjoy, in a sadistic sort of way, having people emotionally in debt to us, so we stretch out the payment plan for as long as possible. If we are successful, we can still bring up the injury, sometimes years after the offense, and squeeze another dime of remorse out of our designated villain.

Forgiveness curtails this sadistic merriment and tells our offenders, "You no longer owe me anything. The debt is forgotten; I no longer expect you to make things right."

The pain of disappointment and disillusionment from a relationship with a chameleon can run deep. As long as the thought of the chameleon or our relationship with him squeezes our hearts, creating feelings of anger and bitterness, he owns the deed to our emotional and spiritual life. When we refuse to forgive, we push God out of our lives and allow the chameleon to remain. We need to forgive more for our sake than for the sake of the other.

When we struggle to forgive, we don't need a touch from God's spiritual wand so that we can magically forgive someone who doesn't deserve it. Instead we need to pray that God will show us how much we need His forgiveness and how much we have been forgiven. If we have witnessed the action of the chameleon and responded we would never live that way, James reminds us, "For whoever shall keep the whole law, and yet stumble in one point, he is guilty of all" (James 2:10).

One evening I was watching an old episode of the "Honeymooners," with Jackie Gleason and Art Carney. As you may recall, the main character, Ralph, drove buses for a living, and his friend Norton worked in the New York sewers. In this show Ralph and Norton had slipped out of the house for an evening on the town and were getting home late. Faced with the problem of sneaking back into their houses without their wives seeing them, Norton suggested that they simply drop into the sewer pipes and come up in their backyards. Ralph wasn't too excited but was desperate and agreed.

As they sloshed through knee-high waste, Norton wasn't bothered at all; he was used to it. Ralph, however, was about to go crazy. He slipped and went completely under the muck, and when he came up, all kinds of things were hanging on him. Overcome with revulsion, he ran the rest of the way home, raced through the front door, up the stairs, through the living room, and into the shower, hardly noticing his wife standing by the bed. Nothing else mattered except getting rid of that filth.

Most of us feel about sin in our lives, the way Norton felt about the sewer. We have lived in it for so long and smelled it so much that we hardly blink when we are knee-deep in it. God, however, wants us to respond to sin as Ralph did to the sewer, to be so repulsed when we come in contact with it that nothing matters except getting to the shower and washing it off. If we ever understand how much we need God's forgiveness, we will no longer struggle to forgive others. We need to be more concerned with our own sin, and less obsessed with others'; more aware of the things that are hanging off of us and how we smell, and less aware of what is hanging off of others.

In Matthew 6:14–15 Jesus said, "For if you forgive men their trespasses, your heavenly Father will also forgive you. But if you do not forgive men their trespasses, neither will your Father forgive your trespasses." God does not suggest that we forgive others; He commands it. We need the forgiveness of God through His Son if we are to be holy and acceptable in God's sight. If we cut ourselves off from that forgiveness by not forgiving others, we distance ourselves from God.

Counterfeit Forgiveness

Knowing that you need to forgive another is different from the actual process—and that's what forgiveness is, a process. Many of us see forgiveness as a onetime decision, an event, a point of choice, and don't recognize that we have a host of emotions—anger, bitterness, sadness—that have resulted from the hurt. Because of this lack of perception, we often give counterfeit forgiveness to the other person, not realizing that we have committed a fraudulent act that will not heal us or satisfy God. There are several kinds of bogus forgiveness.

Selective Forgiveness

We are often selective in our forgiveness of a spouse or long-term friend who has committed a significant number of wrongs against us. I may say, "I can forgive you for this, this, and this, but I can't bring myself to forgive you for that." The implication is that for every five things forgiven, one freebie is allowed. Many times the one thing that can't be forgiven has to do with how I feel about myself. Has the hurtful act diminished our self-image or worth? If the offense touches our pride, it is difficult to forgive.

A wife may forgive her husband for being lazy, addicted to alcohol, even physically abusive to her. But she may not forgive the time he wrote the most beautiful love letter and told her how much he missed her while he was on that business trip. She won't because she later found out that while he was writing that letter a woman he was having an affair with sat in the same room with him. "I can forgive everything but his lying to me," the wife will say.

Consider for a moment a relationship with God based on selective forgiveness, where we weren't sure what God would forgive and what He would not. It would be frightening, indeed, if each time we did something that diminished people's perceptions and feelings about Him we ran the risk of not being forgiven.

Circumstantial Forgiveness

Sometimes we forgive depending on how well things are going in our lives. I may respond, "Hey, I'm doing great and I feel good about myself and my future; but you don't look so good. Oh, you poor thing, of course I forgive you." If, however, life has been treating me like a used foam cup and you like fine china, then forget it; I'm not going to give you one more good thing.

We may take personal or spiritual pride in being able to forgive someone if our feelings of self-worth and accomplishment are positive. Yet the very act may be just a way for us to let the other person know how well we are doing. We can use forgiveness to express an almost arrogant sympathy. If we are still recovering from a wound, feeling "on top" can, of course, be a pleasurable experience.

Love is not a feeling, but an action—something we choose to do. The same can be said of forgiveness. If our forgiveness is based upon how we feel about ourselves or the other person at a particular moment, then our forgiveness will last only as long as the emotion.

User-Friendly Forgiveness

This most widely employed type of forgiveness becomes a tool for manipulation. We often expect that our forgiving or asking forgiveness will improve the quality of our relationship with others, that there will be some positive response: either they will realize how they have wronged us, or they will appreciate our attitude, at least acknowledge that we are trying to do the right thing. Basically, we hope that they will think better of us than before (or that we will be able to think better of them).

Forgiveness loses its salt when we attach expectations to it. Genuine forgiveness is unconditional. Christ's forgiveness is; therefore, ours must be. Anything less is using forgiveness as a bribe to manipulate another person's attitude or action toward us.

Forgiveness changes the direction of a relationship. That forgiveness is not an end point, a finish to the unwanted action or attitude that has been affecting the relationship. We believe that forgiveness resolves the problem that created the need. If this were true, would Christ have us forgive our enemies seventy times seven?

A woman married to a spiritual chameleon, trying to survive in the marriage with the above expectations should not be surprised when bitterness is the result. She begins to see the marriage as an if/then proposition. "If I forgive often enough, if I ask forgiveness often enough, if I respond with love often enough, then he will see Christ's love in me and change." When the gift of forgiveness is continuously refused and despised we feel betrayed. We begin to see ourselves as helpless victims, and the root of bitterness grows, not only against chameleons, but also against God.

Intellectual Forgiveness

Intellectual forgiveness is concerned with appearances, with doing the right thing. I am a Christian, I am supposed to forgive; it is the right and logical thing to do, so I forgive you. Sometimes I call this "Mr. Spock" forgiveness.

I once owned a horse. It was a good trail horse, but it balked at crossing streams. It would walk calmly up to the stream, hesitate for a moment, and then jump the width of the stream with one bound. After several half-gainers into these streams, I decided to get off and lead the horse across. I had waded halfway across the next stream when I felt a momentary tension on the reins just before a 1500-pound flying horse landed on me.

With intellectual forgiveness the mind takes the lead and does the right thing. The heart follows dutifully behind until it gets to a place that it's not emotionally ready to cross. Then the issue that we thought was behind us grabs the heart and knocks us flat.

When Karen's husband left her for another woman, she was emotionally devastated. Through that loss, however, and with the support of a Christian friend, she gave her life to Jesus Christ. Two years after the divorce Karen was a stable, growing Christian. Her husband had remarried and Karen believed she had come to terms with it and forgiven him. She had custody of the children, but visitation rights allowed him to see them every other weekend.

One Sunday morning, during the worship service, Karen looked up to see her ex-husband, his wife, and her two children sitting a couple of pews in front of her. During the entire service she watched her children and the man who should have been her own husband, sitting with another woman in her place. It took almost two months for Karen to begin recovering from what she had seen. The emotional upheaval of anger and bitterness, feelings she thought she had put behind her, swept over her life like a tidal wave.

In her mind Karen had forgiven her husband, but that Sunday morning her heart, which had been quietly following behind, leapt ahead, dragging her down a trail she thought she had traveled for the last time two years earlier. Karen learned that day that forgiveness—like spiritual maturity—is a process. We seldom know how far we've come, or how far we've got to go, until time, people, and circumstances flow across the bridge of that forgiveness and test how strong we are.

We know we have truly forgiven the chameleon when we see that person through the filter of Christ's love and not the mask of our own hurt. The more often we come into contact with that person, without our blood pressure going up and our spiritual discernment going down, the more complete is our forgiveness. We will once again want the best for the chameleon. We may someday begin to minister to the chameleon in whatever capacity the Lord allows us, perhaps even directly impact his life in some way. Until then, it may be all we can do to pray for the chameleon. But as we are willing to intercede in their lives for the sake of Christ, God is ready and willing to bless our lives.

One afternoon I watched a professional dog trainer work with a hunting dog that loved to chase rabbits. The trainer put an electric shock collar around the dog's neck. The collar had a boxlike receiver on the outside, and two small metal prongs on the inside, against the dog's neck. The trainer held a control that sent an electric shock to the dog when a button was pressed. The trainer watched closely as the dog worked out in the field. If the dog began to chase a rabbit and ignored the whistle to stop and return, the trainer would give him an electric shock.

For someone having no knowledge of the collar, the animal's behavior would seem bizarre. First, the dog was a happy-go-lucky animal, tail wagging, nose to the ground, having a good time running around in the field. Suddenly, it would do a half-flip into the air and let out an agonized yelp, as it raced around in tight circles, trying to get at whatever was biting it on the neck.

When we have not forgiven people, and remain emotionally tied to them, they have the same control over us as that trainer had over the dog. When we least expect it—when we are enjoying a conversation, having a quiet time with the Lord, or simply daydreaming—we may remember what that person did to us and respond as if we had a shock collar attached to our hearts. We yelp and do a spiritual flip when a memory pushes the button.

A woman in our ministry told me that during her marriage she and her husband owned an almond farm. One spring afternoon while they were walking in the orchard, he told her that he was leaving her for another woman. "Terry," she said, "to this day, every time I drive through the country and the almond trees are in blossom, just the smell of those trees makes the bitterness and anger boil up all over again. It's like he's able to reach out and grab my soul, and we've been divorced for over four years."

Forgiveness unbuckles and removes that emotional shock collar that hurt and betrayal put there.

The chameleon can leave spiritual devastation in his wake. No one else can leave such a feeling of betrayal, or so effectively undermine one's faith in fellow believers. The question is, once he leaves are you going to allow him to continue blinding you with the afterglow of his colors?

The spiritual chameleon is not some alien from another world. He or she is a person caught up and drowning in deceit, which the curse of original sin produces in us all. Romans 3:23 says, "For all have sinned and fall short of the glory of God." That makes all of us chameleons; we can't help ourselves. The issue of the chameleon is not whether or not you are one, but to what degree has this kind of deceit invaded your spiritual life.

Before you go out hunting chameleons, or looking for reasons to forgive them, it might be a good idea to run your own life through the filter of this book. You may come away hoping that those who have come into contact with you have the capacity to forgive.

Chapter 11

RESTORING THE COLORS

SECOND CORINTHIANS 5:18 SAYS, "Now all things are of God, who has reconciled us to Himself through Jesus Christ, and has given us the ministry of reconciliation." We have the ministry of reconciling people to God—people who have never met Him; people who have met Him, but walked away; people who don't know Him as well as they pretend. In Jim's book *Reconcilable Differences,* he defines reconciliation as "a process of causing once more to be friendly, to bring back the harmony." When we help to reconcile people to God, whatever their spiritual circumstances, we make it possible for them to experience joy at being in harmony with their Creator and His plan for their lives.

Confrontation: the Beginning of Restoration

When we share Christ with a nonbeliever and he invites Jesus into his life, we have helped begin for him a lifelong process of reconciliation to God.

As we share with others, the first step is to promote an awareness of the need for God. We share about how God has changed our lives. We stir the desire in them for similar changes. Hopefully we clarify God's holiness and righteousness, how sinful we are, and that Jesus Christ is the only bridge to a relationship with God. By sharing Christ we confront them with the truth about themselves and about God, and give them an opportunity to make a choice.

Sharing Christ is the process of confrontation. It is probably the ultimate confrontation. When we share Christ we do not judge or sentence; we clarify some basic spiritual issues, assure others that they do have a choice, then share the choice we made when confronted with that same truth. Jim Elliot said, "Father make me a crisis man. Let me not be a milepost on a single road. Make me a fork that men must turn one way or another on facing Christ in me."

Confrontation is not judging, but clarifying and sharing choices. It is not the process of tearing down and destroying, but of nourishing an awareness of a problem, and offering help and support in dealing with that problem.

Confrontation begins with the premise that a person is free to change and pursue a different course. Confrontation supposes that forgiveness has already taken place and that there is no condemnation, only concern and optimism that restoration is a possibility.

Scripture says, "Preach the word! Be ready in season and out of season. Convince, rebuke, exhort, with all longsuffering and teaching" (2 Tim. 4:2). In other words, when done according to Scripture, confrontation is part of the process of restoration. *Reprove* comes from the Greek word *elencho* which means to clarify; to expose to the light. *To rebuke* means to say what is wrong. Once you have pointed out the wrong path, you must explain why it is wrong; the heart must be convicted. A person often is not even aware that there are spiritual issues in his or her life that need to change. Sometimes we are oblivious to subtle sin, which can have a most serious impact on our relationship with Christ or with others. Thus, we need people in our lives who will continue to reconcile us to God through sharing the truth about Christ with us.

A few years ago I was experiencing a period of spiritual dryness. I didn't feel like praying; I was going through the motions during my quiet time; it had been months since I shared with anyone the joy of my salvation, mainly because I felt very little joy. I shared this struggle with two men who have the freedom to jump around in my life and bang on me as much as they care to: One is Jim Talley, my pastor, and therefore my spiritual authority; the other is Dennis Shaeffer who is my intimate friend.

I am very fortunate to have both of these men in my life, because they come at issues from completely different but equally valid directions. Jim is a functional leader whose objective tendencies—toward goals, structure, and programming—have been softened by the Holy Spirit's constant washing with love, patience, and sensitivity. He asked me questions, first about ministry, then about my job. Ministry was going well; my job was another issue. My administrator and I could not agree on several issues concerning the operation of the school. Having been there fifteen years, I felt that many of my ideas were not only valid but essential in their implementation.

Jim then asked me some very simple questions. Who was superintendent of the school? I responded with the administrator's name. Who was my boss? Rather impatiently, I pronounced his name again. He then asked if this man had authority over me in all areas pertaining to the school, and I said yes. Who put him in authority over me? With a deep sigh, I said God, thinking of Romans 13:1–2: "Let every soul be subject to the governing authorities. For there is no authority except from God, and the authorities that exist are appointed by God. Therefore whoever resists the authority resists the ordinance of God, and those who resist will bring judgment on themselves."

The bottom line was that I had a rebellious spirit when it came to my job and my boss. It was not that I couldn't express a difference of opinion or give input, but that I had neither the responsibility nor authority to make decisions. Once those decisions had been made, by a man whom God had put in authority over me, I needed to submit, with a willing and supportive heart, to whatever the decision might be.

Jim had reproved me by clarifying the issue of authority in my life. He then exhorted and encouraged me to go to my administrator and ask forgiveness.

A few days later I was sharing the same issues with Dennis. Dennis is very relational and subjective, but I have noticed in him an ability to understand a person's feelings while maintaining enough objectivity to help that person sort out those feelings and deal with them.

He was asking questions of me when the issue of my administrator came up. His questions came from the relational perspective. He asked questions such as how do you feel about this man? What are some good things you can tell me about him? Do you love this man? Just as with Jim, Dennis sought to clarify the problem, helping me to understand my feelings about my boss, the flaw in those feelings, and encouraging me to keep Philippians 4:8 in mind when thinking of him.

It is important to open your life to spiritual authority and to people who are close to you. Both men addressed the same issue from different perspectives because the gifts and insights the Holy Spirit had given them were filtered through different personalities and life experiences. But both men were correct and I was able to gain twice the insight, because God spoke to me through two men instead of one.

Throughout the process of clarification, conviction, and encouragement, I realized that my spiritual dryness was a direct result of a rebellious spirit. I had ongoing, unconfessed sin in my life, and it was creating a barrier between God and me. Looking back I can see that even I was fooled by the manifestation of my chameleon nature. My beautiful, spiritually submissive colors, which I wore within the ministry at church, blinded me to the fact that I was an ornery, rebellious employee, not trusting God enough outside of the ministry structure to be a submissive servant.

After doing what was asked of me by both Jim and Dennis I noticed that the spiritual dimension of my life almost immediately changed. I looked forward to prayer, especially prayer about my attitude on the job. My quiet time took on a warmth and intimacy, which had been missing, and God's Word spoke to me once more. Naturally, my relationship with my administrator improved significantly, and through this experience I was able to share with him what Christ was doing in my life. Through the confrontational process I had been reconciled with Christ, and my relationship with Him had been restored.

Clarification: Do You See What I See?

Clarification is usually the most difficult part of the confrontational process unless the person opens himself as I did with Jim and Dennis. Creating awareness of a problem without appearing judgmental requires sensitivity and vulnerability. Sharing with other believers the struggles and failures in our lives allows them to face similar issues in their lives without losing their sense of spiritual worth.

It had been a miserable two days. My first evaluation by my new principal was excellent; I enjoyed the new Sunday school class I was teaching and it was growing, but I was still miserable. I had received a mysterious tax refund of fifty dollars on my home owner's loan; my wife had committed herself to less TV and more prayer and reading of the Word. She was on a spiritual high: That was why it had been a miserable two days.

I didn't start out miserable; at first I was just irritated. When she tactfully suggested that there were some shows on TV that made her uncomfortable, I nodded and added in a contrite tone that she was absolutely right, and that I would be happy to move the television set to one of the back bedrooms the next day. My well-hidden irritation arose from two things: I hadn't suggested it first—I hadn't even thought of it—and now I was going to miss some of my favorite shows.

The irritation drifted into exasperation over the next several days. I had developed what I considered an efficient and quite effective quiet time. It was usually tacked on to my teaching preparation time, or picked up each morning during my drive to work through downtown traffic. I tried having it in the evening, but it was rather difficult to schedule it around the *TV Guide* listings. I gave early morning a try, but I'm not a morning person, so who could expect me to stay awake when it was so quiet?

Jo Ann, of course, had to have her quiet time smack-dab in the middle of my morning. And this wasn't just any quiet time; no, it had real delusions of grandeur. I mean she actually sat there for thirty to forty-five minutes praying and reading the Word, insinuating that one couldn't have a spiritually meaningful time in the flow of traffic on McHenry Avenue.

Of course, while one person is having a quiet time in the house, the other person needs to be quiet as well. I like to do a lot of banging and muttering and grunting that first hour or so, but who can grunt and mutter in any meaningful way with the equivalent of Mother Teresa sitting in the next room?

The next morning I went outside and "accidentally" dropped the garbage can while running the garage door up and down, but I found little solace in this, especially when I returned to the house and, with a sweet smile, Jo Ann thanked me for putting the garbage out.

Although vexation rolled around inside of me like a third degree sunburn, in front of Jo Ann I was the mature, caring, spiritual support system I was supposed to be. Not for her, mind you; her needs during that time were about as important to me as a bucket of whale spit. No, I was concerned for myself, for my image as the Christian husband caring for his Christian wife as Christ cares for the church.

During the past year I had become very conscious of my image as a leader in the church, and while at church or with friends I had taken on the appropriate spiritual colors: I had become a spiritual chameleon. At home my colors were unnecessary until Jo Ann changed the background on which I was sitting. I suddenly found my plain, boring spiritual shade somewhat embarrassing when contrasted with the bright hue of my wife's devotion to personal spiritual growth.

Irritation and annoyance do not find their feeding ground in being uncomfortable with others. Instead, they are nurtured by being ill at ease with yourself. Although I'm fairly slow about these things I realized that Jo Ann wasn't the problem; the problem was with me, a man who loved the Lord dearly but for a few months had pretended that love had changed him more than it really had.

When Jo Ann shared the reason for her recommitment to her relationship with Christ, she said that because of her functional position in ministry as a coordinator of women's care groups, she was finding it easy to give the impression that her walk with Christ was all that it should be. She allowed it to happen though she was aware that her prayer life and personal time with God were not satisfactory.

Scripture says that the two shall become as one. As a spiritual leader in our home I was not necessarily making wrong decisions, but I had allowed our spiritual growth as a couple to slow to a pace which was uncomfortable for my spouse. We were using ministry positions to gloss over the drabness of our walk with Christ with the bright, impressive colors of our titles.

When Jo Ann shared her feelings about these things, she was concerned that what had happened in her life was also happening in mine. But throughout the entire conversation she did not mention me once. The issue was her life, not mine; what Jo Ann was going to do, not what she thought I should do. She allowed me to look into the mirror of her life and see the spiritual struggles she was having, that the reflection might cast some light upon my life and let me see myself clearly. I had been confronted with the false colors in my life in the gentlest, most desirable way possible: the example of another.

Winston Churchill said, "Men occasionally stumble over the truth, but most of them pick themselves up and hurry off as if nothing happened." The truth was plain. I knew that my prayer time and quiet time were not what they should be. I knew that I was not encouraging Jo Ann in her walk. I knew all of this and more, but chose to ignore it, especially since my spiritual colors looked good to those who had no occasion to suspect differently. Jo Ann's struggle and change of direction had clarified the same issue for me in my life. I believe most of us willfully ignore the obvious until something slides across the path of our lives and prompts us to move in a different direction.

Many of us choose to disregard the examples of others' lives, examples God provides for us so that we may see our own more clearly, as Jo Ann did for me. Some of us even choose to ignore God's willingness to deal with us directly, as Jim and Dennis did with me. We float along rationalizing that things are not as bad as they appear.

My Soft and Gentle Journey of Deceit

In C. S. Lewis's *Screwtape Letters* one senior devil, Screwtape, is advising an apprentice devil on the most effective way to move Christ off the throne of our lives: "Remember, Wormwood, the only thing that matters is the extent to which you separate the man from God. It does not matter how small the sins are provided that when they are added up the effect is to edge the man away from the light and out into the searing cold of nothingness. Murder is no better than bitterness, if bitterness can do the trick. Indeed the safest road away from God is the gradual one. The gentle slope, soft underfoot, without sudden turnings, without great events, without signposts. Suddenly you reach a destination not planned but so easily arrived at."

The chameleon's path is probably the most subtle because it is camouflaged so well. We wind ourselves up in a maze of half-truths, rationalizations, and deceit until nothing seems able to penetrate the disguise. But God's love does not allow Him to give up on us, and though we may stubbornly choose to live in a spiritual prison for years, God will eventually say enough, and through people and circumstances bring us to a place where we can no longer keep up this facade of spiritual color. He clarifies our sin through the most painful process of all, but many times the only one that we have left to Him: suffering the consequences of the sin we chose for so long to ignore.

For twelve years I sat in that prison, with my first wife, Kathy, wearing the colors of a spiritual leader in my church and home until one evening the colors began to fade and the consequences gripped my life. The face of the woman who sat in the overstuffed chair across from me was quite familiar. I had known it for twelve years and had seen almost every emotion imaginable come to life on that face, with the exception of what I saw now. The small, delicate mouth and button nose were the same. The wispy blond hair still fell in ringlets across her forehead; but I didn't recognize the eyes. They were a blank page, focused on something that was not a part of me or the room, something that now separated us in an ominous way.

As she spoke I was amazed at the tone, which matched her eyes perfectly. She sat rigidly, almost like a stick figure, perched on the chair instead of sitting in it. There were no nervous mannerisms, not the slightest swing of a foot or tap of a finger.

"I am going to leave you. I don't love you anymore, at least, not in the way that I should, and I must leave. I have thought about this for a long time and there is no point in trying to change my mind."

As I began to speak I had the strange feeling that my words somehow floated between us.

They were neither accepted nor rejected, just simply not acknowledged. From that point forward the dialogue was like a script with the outcome fixed. There was nothing I could do, say, or promise that would have any effect on the twelve years of unanswered expectations and granitelike bitterness that grew out of those disappointments.

Any Christian who's been around the block will tell you that this was the best thing that could have happened to me, a kind of spiritual open-heart surgery. Depression, however, was a new experience for me.

Because my emotional stability took a sudden nosedive, my loving and forgiving nature took a sharp left turn. My pain drove me to levels of absurdity. I had an intense and malicious desire to see Kathy suffer more than I had; the villains should always suffer more. I spent the next three days screaming and yelling at God about the twisted logic in life and the definite lack of fairness in the universe.

As I sat there in exhausted repose, having straightened God out, a still, small voice began to whisper to me. It reminded me of the many times Kathy had wanted to talk and I had refused to listen, of my obsession with scheduling my life around television, fishing, and duck hunting and expecting her to compete for whatever was left. She had never had the opportunity to be my friend and knew little of my cares and fears. In twelve years she had never seen me cry. She had lived in a black and white, two-dimensional life with me, catching the colors of what might have been only on Sunday or during a Wednesday night Bible study. The process of clarification had begun.

After about three days and nights of this "still, small voice" screaming in my ear, I felt a weariness that squeezed the fabric of my being. Had I not been a Christian I could have rationalized my way out of the marriage, but I could see clearly that this was not an acceptable option to God. I had sinned against Kathy and against God. God entered my life on His conditions, not mine, and I was just beginning to understand what some of those conditions were.

The first was that the Holy Spirit was part of me. Over the last two weeks He had made His presence undeniably clear. The next condition I was dismally beginning to understand was there was no way of dismissing Him. The more I tried to escape, the more overwhelmed I became at the futility of it all. God had lived in my heart as a stranger for twelve years. I knew Him only as someone who had brought a gift and lived in one of the back rooms of my heart.

There was one thing I understood clearly: Jesus Christ was working in my life and even in the midst of my confused misery, there was a subtle excitement that tinged that realization. He was encouraging me to step toward Him. At the beginning of this ordeal I was under the hopeful illusion that there would be a time limit to all of this. As time passed, however, I realized that sticking my thumb in my mouth, rolling up in a fetal position, and waiting for the tide to go out was not the answer. Instead of screaming and yelling at Him, or whimpering in a corner, I had to move. At least with movement it was possible to change direction.

The final step in this process of reconciliation to God, and restoration to the body of Christ, came in the form of a man named Dave Forrest. Dave had stepped in when Kathy had stepped out. He had become my friend, my Christian friend. His care was simply his availability, his counsel was his determination to help me find answers in the Word of God, to share some of his own mistakes, and assure me that mine were not unforgivable. He was part of the most important step in the restoration process: to support and encourage.

Many people believe that confrontation is simply telling someone: "Don't do that anymore!" What makes confrontation such a serious business is that if you are willing to confront, then you must be willing to help that person change, and this can be a long, involved process. Dave was willing to meet with me for over a year, every Wednesday morning. There were others who stepped into my life and taught me, discipled me, befriended me, and challenged me. In the process they revealed their true colors to me. I no longer felt intimidated or pressured to be who I was not. I felt loved and accepted for who I was, a child of God. And that was the key to the spiritual restoration of Terry Benner.

I had met people who were willing to be honest and spiritually vulnerable with me, sharing that God had been truly gracious and patient with them, just as He would be gracious and patient with me.

Closing the Theater

Danny couldn't believe how good he felt. He didn't feel good because he had remembered all of his lines or because his teacher seemed very proud or because his mother had given him a big hug and his dad had shaken his hand; he felt good because it was finally over. The school play was behind him. He was amazed as he lay there in bed that night at how good the future looked now that the play had become part of the past. Once again, he could relax and be himself. Danny went to sleep that night with a smile on his face.

I believe, as Shakespeare said, that all of the world is a stage. From the time we are small, we are taught to be actors and actresses—to play a part, to fill a role, to make sure we know our lines. Very few people, if any, see or know the real us. We are taught that people are watching; there is always an audience who is judging our performance.

We spend our lives feeling the glare of the spotlight and, at the best of times, hearing the applause—at the worst of times, the boos and jeers. But we are always living between the possibility of those two responses. Unlike Danny, we are never able to relax and go to sleep with a smile on our face because the play spans our entire life; that is unless, of course, the manager of the theater is a personal friend of ours who has the power to shut off the lights and tell the audience to go home.

When I invited Christ into my life, the first thing I felt was the white–hot glare of those lights being turned off. As the lights lost their brilliance, I could gradually look down from the stage and see that those seats, those thousands of seats, were empty. I felt Christ putting His arm around me and leading me from the stage, and I heard Him say, "Terry, the performance is over. You can relax now. You no longer have to worry about forgetting your lines, putting on your costume, or remembering your cues.

"The play will continue, but you're not going to be part of it. You are now a part of my family, and in my family acting is not necessary or even allowed. Audiences have no value. There is no longer anything to prove or anything to earn.

" 'Come to Me, all who are weary and heavy-laden, and I will give you rest. Take My yoke upon you, and learn from Me, for I am gentle and humble in heart; and you shall find rest for your souls. For My yoke is easy, and My load is light' " (Matt. 11:28–30, NAS).

As Danny had, I went to sleep that night with a smile on my face because the play was a thing of the past and I was now free.

Freedom in Christ is freedom from being on the stage of the world and continually trying to please an audience that can never be satisfied. When the chameleon begins to penetrate our spiritual lives for whatever reason, we step back onstage, move under the lights, and begin to invite the audience back to their seats.

Each night, just like Danny, we need to remind ourselves that the play is over; there is no need to change colors to blend in with the scenery, use fake props or special effects. Then comes the peaceful joy and, of course, the smile.